HANDS-ON AFRICA

ART ACTIVITIES FOR ALL AGES
FEATURING SUB-SAHARAN AFRICA

This book is dedicated to Judith Keller, her husband Nelson Cronyn and sons Max and Avery who live in Niger and are working to build a better West Africa. Here are Judith and Max with their friends Yasine and Ashiot in Namey, Niger. Their and their colleagues' interest and help with this book are appreciated.

Book design by Art & International Productions, LLC, Anchorage, Alaska
Laurel Casjens took the photographs.
Mary Simpson illustrated the book and assisted with the development of the crafts.
Emily Mortensen and Madlyn Tanner edited and proofread the text.

Other books by the author
from KITS Publishing:

Hands-on Africa
(ISBN 0-9643177-7-X)

Hands-on Alaska
(ISBN 0-9643177-3-7)

Hands-on Asia
(ISBN 0-9643177-5-3)

Hands-on Celebrations
(ISBN 0-9643177-4-5)

Hands-on Rocky Mountains
(ISBN 0-9643177-2-9)

Hands-on Latin America
(ISBN 0-9643177-1-0)

Hands-on Pioneers*
(ISBN 1-57345-085-5)

KITS PUBLISHING
2359 E. Bryan Avenue   Salt Lake City, Utah 84108
(801) 582-2517   fax: (801) 582-2540
e-mail - info@hands-on.com   web - www.hands-on.com
*Published by Deseret Book

Library of Congress Control Number 00-131069
ISBN 0-9643177-7-X

(Opposite page) The Yungai family and Kayla Dickenson are in front of the Ndebele housefront mural on the title page.
They are Ashanti, Sakile, Nzingha, Ola and Osai.

HANDS-ON AFRICA

ART ACTIVITIES FOR ALL AGES
FEATURING SUB-SAHARAN AFRICA

YVONNE Y. MERRILL
KITS PUBLISHING

TABLE OF CONTENTS

AN INTRODUCTION TO AFRICAN ART

Africa is one of the largest continents in the world and home to hundreds of varieties of ethnic people and many ecosystems from jungle to desert. The earliest evidence of man is found in African soil and caves. Most of us think of exotic animals and safaris when we think of Africa. But Africa, today and yesterday, is also rich in art and design. Household furnishings from 3100 B.C. and colorful kente' cloth from 1000 A.D. are all indications of the important role of artistic expression and craftsmanship that has been traditional since earliest civilizations.

Today, African art is a blend of historical and contemporary styles. Art objects are ceremonial or practical, created to contribute to community life. Folk and fine art are cataloged in one of these categories.

Body Adornment

Sculpture

Textiles

Woodcarving

Masks

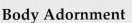

Artifacts of ancient Africa indicate that great civilizations thrived 8,000 years ago. Imaginative cave art in the Matopa hills and the Sahara Desert reveal attention to aesthetics and design. The Nubians in the Sudan, the Ife who taught the Benin artisans metal and sculpting techniques, the intellectual center at Timbuktu, and the religious importance of the renowned mosque, Djenne (Jenne'), are traces of early civilization. Arabs explored the East coast and introduced the Islam faith as well as art styles. By 1100 A.D. Great Zimbabwe in Southeastern Africa was a trade center for gold, ivory, and slaves, exposing African people to art and traditions from other places.

Sahara

Timbuktu

Sudan

Djenne

Benin

Matopa

In 1487 Bartholomew Diaz rounded Cape Horn and made the first European contact with Africa. Ten years later in 1497 Vasco da Gama sailed to India and forged new trade routes. Diego Cao explored the Congo River, claiming the drainage area for Portugal. From the 17th Century to 1889 more than 20 million African people were forced into slavery. Today, many areas of modern Africa struggle with civil war, depleted soil, the Aids disease, political upheaval, and human rights issues. Art continues to be an important means of expression often adapted to plastics, glass, and new materials.

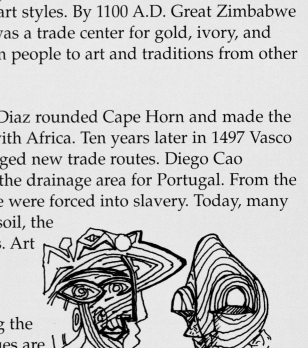

African art has influenced many modern styles, including the art of Pablo Picasso and Henri Matisse. Cubism techniques are credited to African origins. Abstractionism, a style with body-part proportions enlarged and reduced, finds its beginnings in African art.

Introduction to African Map

20 important features in Sub-Saharan Africa to locate on the map

Africa is the second largest continent in the world. It covers an area of nearly 12 million square miles. It is roughly triangular in shape, with the Mediterranean Sea to the north, the Atlantic Ocean to the west, and the Indian Ocean to the east. Africa has 50 nations with 10% of the world's population. There are 900 ethnic groups on the continent. Africa is rich in resources, fascinating ancient sites, geographical wonders, and historical places. Match the places with the numbers on the map.

1. Bushmen

2. Diamond mines

3. Kalahari desert

4. Matopa hills

5. Table Mountain

6. Okuvanga swamp

7. Great Zimbabwe

8. Madagascar lemur

9. Zanzibar

10. Safari country

11. Mt. Kilimanjaro

12. Copper mines

13. Victoria Falls

14. Church of the Cross

15. The Congo River

16. Slave castles

17. Ancient Kilwa

18. Timbuktu

19. Jenné Mosque

20. Benin

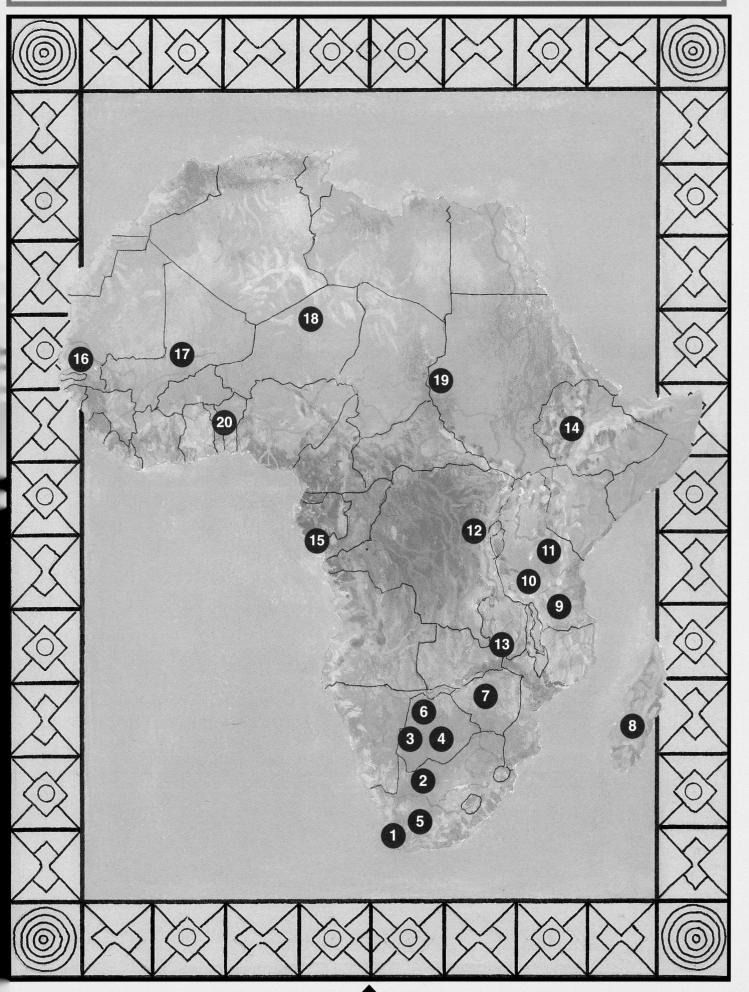

WEST AFRICA

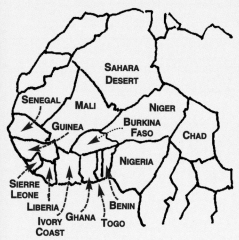

The political boundaries of West Africa were formed just over 100 years ago. Still, they mean little to the map of West African tribal groups that traversed the open land for centuries.

Archeological evidence indicates that an upright hominid existed in Africa nearly 4 million years ago. Other evidence reveals that possibly 750,000 years ago people were using large stone axes for hunting.

The Sahara was once a place of rainfall and grasses 10,000 years before the Ice Age ended. The production of iron tools (450 B.C.) made it possible to clear forests. Iron weaponry allowed stronger tribes to conquer and absorb weaker groups.

TRANS-SAHARAN TRADE: West African traders crossed the Sahara to northern Africa and Mediterranean ports, exporting salt, gold, slaves, silver, and ivory. Islam was founded in Arabia by Prophet Mohammed around 620 A.D. Converts moved south and the new religion was adopted by the rich and powerful. Common people retained their animistic religions. Today West Africa is a blend of traditional religions, Islam and Christianity.

MALI: By the 14th Century the Mali Empire controlled nearly all the sub-Saharan trade. Timbuktu became a learning and financial center in 1324 after Emperor Mansu Musa visited Mecca and returned with reknowned Arab scholars. The Songhai became powerful 100 years later and built the great mosque at Jenné. Today it is of architectural and historical interest to visitors. Several thriving empires existed: the Hausa and Kanem-Bomo in the Lake Chad region; the Benin in Nigeria; and the Dahomey, Mossi, and Ashanti in Ghana. Many remain today with century-old traditions of art, sculpture, and textiles.

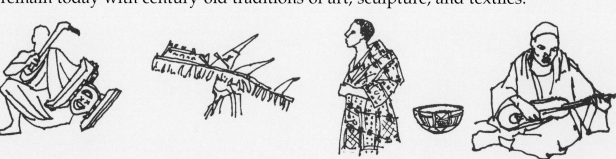

carved wooden stools   a ritual mask   kenté cloth robe   etched gourd bowl   a four-string lute

The Portuguese were the first Europeans to explore the African coast, and their exploration flourished from 1795 to 1850. Many of the explorers were searching for the fabled city of gold, Timbuktu, and the source of the Nile River (which was finally determined in 1828). The 19th Century was marked by colonization. Ghana became the first independent colony in 1957. Most of Africa has become independent since then, changing names and systems of government as the turbulent events unfold. Some distinct cultural groups are:

THE BAMBARA of Mali have generally lived around the drainage of the Niger River. Great trading centers were common. The Bambara carved the Chi Wara antelope masks, passing the skill from father to son. The mud cloth resist textiles were also traditionally made by the women.

THE TUAREGS are descended from the Berbers who fled south from North Africa. They are called "the blue people of the desert" because of their indigo-dyed blue robes, the color often rubbing off on their skin. The Tuareg women wear impressive quantities of jewelry, paint their faces, and are known for their painted leatherwork.

THE FULANI herd cattle and also wear their personal wealth. The women wear oversized gold earrings, often weighing 3 to 4 pounds. Jewelry indicates marital status and degree of wealth.

THE DOGON carved doors for their granaries and made fine wooden door posts, prized by collectors.

THE SENUFO on the Ivory Coast painted white cotton fabric with stylized designs of masked figures and abstract animals. Geometric patterns cover Senufo fabric, making handsome wall hangings and pillows which are highly prized by designers. Originally the fabric was made to be worn by the hunter as a good-luck omen.

Fulani Woman

The fiber excellence of kenté cloth, resist fabrics such as mud cloth, and adire eleko are some of West Africa's prized and traditional arts.

DOGON ANIMAL MASK

DOGON ANIMAL MASK

Materials: Newspaper, railroad board 18" x 8", scissors, masking tape, white, maroon, yellow, brown paint and brushes, a Q-tip or pointed tool.

1. Draw this half-face on the fold of your newspaper. Keep the center nose 1/2" at the top to 3/4" at the bottom so it will be wide enough to support the face insert.

2. Trace your cutout pattern onto your cardboard piece. Carefully cut out the two rectangle places that will be the face.

3. Cut a rectangle 5" x 6". Notch the corners 1/2". Fold the notched edge all the way around so you have created a "tray with an edge". Place it against the open back of your cutout face. When you masking tape it onto the mask will it fill the space? Cut out the two round eyeholes after carefully marking them beside the long nose piece.

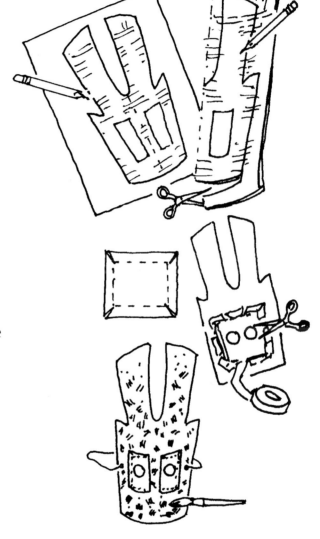

4. Paint your mask using the lighter color on the insert. When the paint has dried, dab the white dots on with a Q-tip or a brush tip. When the paint is dry on the face insert, tape it to the mask back and align the eyeholes.

5. Attach your string for wearing and try on your handsome mask.

The Dogon of Mali wear this mask to celebrate the planting season. The performer wears the mask in an agricultural ceremony and carries a stick for cultivating and weeding the ground. The mask is linked to the dance: gesture, rhythm, and song are important for the total effect. The mask is more than just a face covering. With it are worn raffia collars or skirts, straw woven costumes, or cloth clothing. All of these parts represent the spirit...the dance, song, face covering, and body covering...and are equally important to the meaning to be conveyed. The mask is most important because it is worn on the head, the seat of wisdom, so the mask is given the utmost drama for a powerful effect.

THREE TUAREG CONTAINERS

THREE TUAREG CONTAINERS

Materials: Cardboard, heavy paper, red and black colored paper, fine-tipped markers in red, black, yellow, teal and beige, scissors, glue, a pencil, string, a Styrofoam meat tray, yarn.

Colorful purse

1. Cut two pieces of paper 8″ wide and 5 1/2″ high. With a pencil, section the paper into three equal design areas: one middle and one on each side. The Tuaregs painted on fine leather using these repeat designs. Pencil in your designs on both sides of the bag.
2. Color the designs with fine-tipped markers. Make the 1/2″ paper strips 18″ long. Glue the bottom and edges of the bag together. Glue on the straps as handles.

Round box

1. Cut a strip of manila folder cardboard or railroad board 23″ long and 3″ high. Cut two 4″ circles, one for the lid and one for the box bottom. Cut 3/4″ notches around the edges of each, 1/2″ apart.
2. Lay the strip out and measure varying widths of stripes. Using yellow, red, and teal green color your stripes. Staple or glue the strip ends together. Bend the notches and check your lid for size. It can fit on the inside or outside of the box, depending on its size. Cut a heart pattern. Cut three hearts: one paper and two Styrofoam. Color your designs onto the paper. Glue all the hearts on the lid and color the paper heart. Glue a paper strip around the lid edge to cover up the notches.

Black bag

1. Cut a strip of black paper (the heavier the better) 18″ long and 5″ wide, folding back 4″ for the flap. Make black marker designs on the black paper to give the surface the look of tooled leather.
2. Assemble the bag by gluing the edges. Make fringe with several strips of red and black paper. Staple or glue it to the bag bottom. Add a colorful strip of decorated paper with yarn jutting from the edges. Glue two more yarn decorated strips to the top sides of the pouch. Attach sturdy string to the strips. You now have a Tuareg pouch.

WHIMSICAL SENUFO FIGURES

WHIMSICAL SENUFO FIGURES

Materials: A sheet of Foamie® (@59 cents), scissors, paper and pencil, a sharp-tipped tool, tempera or acrylic paint, brush, paper or fabric, paint tray, water and paper towels for cleanup.

Here are some traditional Senufo figures to give you ideas for your printmaking. Look at the photograph as well.

1. Draw the designed figure on a piece of paper with a pencil. Remember to fill the inside of the figure with pattern.

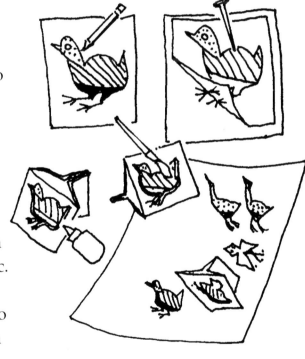

2. Place your drawing on top of the Foamie piece and with a nail or sharp pencil-tip trace the pencil lines onto the Foamie, cutting right through the paper drawing. Lift up the drawing and check that the marks are in the foam. *Be careful not to cut through the foam.* Cut out your figure and mount it on a cardboard strip scored to be a handle.

3. To make a print, try brushing the paint onto the foam and pressing it paint-side down onto the paper or fabric. Slowly rub over the printing foam with your finger. Lift and check the results. Another printing method is to spread the paint onto a paper plate and stamp the foam piece onto the paint and then make a print.

The Senufo are a tribe of people that live in Fakaha, a village on the Ivory Coast in West Africa. The men make the Senufo paintings. Traditionally the figures are drawn with mud paint onto woven white cloth. These were made for hunters to wear for success or for dancing. Human figures are generally portrayed as masked.

Today the Senufo murals are popular tourist items. They are made into pillows, wall hangings, tablecloths, etc.

Good-Luck Charms

GOOD-LUCK CHARMS: GRIS GRIS

Materials: Colored paper and fabric, scissors, glue, pencil, beads, buttons, whimsical cereal, markers, string, yarn or ribbon. A lucky fragment to stuff in pocket. A needle and thread are optional.

Look at the photograph of our sample *gris gris* (gree gree). *Gris gris* are usually made of leather or heavy fabric. They are beaded, decorated with cowrie shells, and usually the shape of a symbolic plant or animal figure from the region. Designs are completely free and mixed.

1. Choose the paper or cloth you are going to use. Gather the decorative pieces such as buttons or beads. We glued our decorations. You may wish to sew them.

2. On a piece of paper draw and cut out a pattern for your gris gris that is 3″x 5″ in size. Lay the pattern onto a folded paper or cloth. Trace around the pattern and cut it out. Be sure and include a tab for attachment.

3. Glue or sew the decorative pieces to the top surface of the *gris gris.* Use markers for additional designs.

4. When the glue is dry insert a good-luck object such as a coin. Glue or sew around the edge.

5. Put a string through the tab and hang it around your neck, belt or in a pocket or bag.

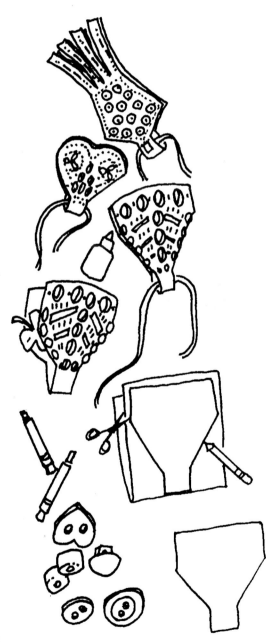

The importance of charms in African cultures has contributed to every aspect of art production. The commonly worn *gris gris* are generally rich in beadwork, leather tooling, and metal design. Some families have had their personal design for generations and these are beaded or incised into the charm. *Gris gris* are any shape, size, or color. They are decorated pouches that hold something that might bring good luck (a lock of hair, a coin, an herb, etc.). *Gris gris* are worn around the neck, the waist, on a belt, or attached to a bag. A person might wear many *gris gris* at once. Any age wears a *gris gris* for protection. Babies wear little *gris gris* as necklaces or tummy belts. A *gris gris* belt would be like a charm bracelet to us.

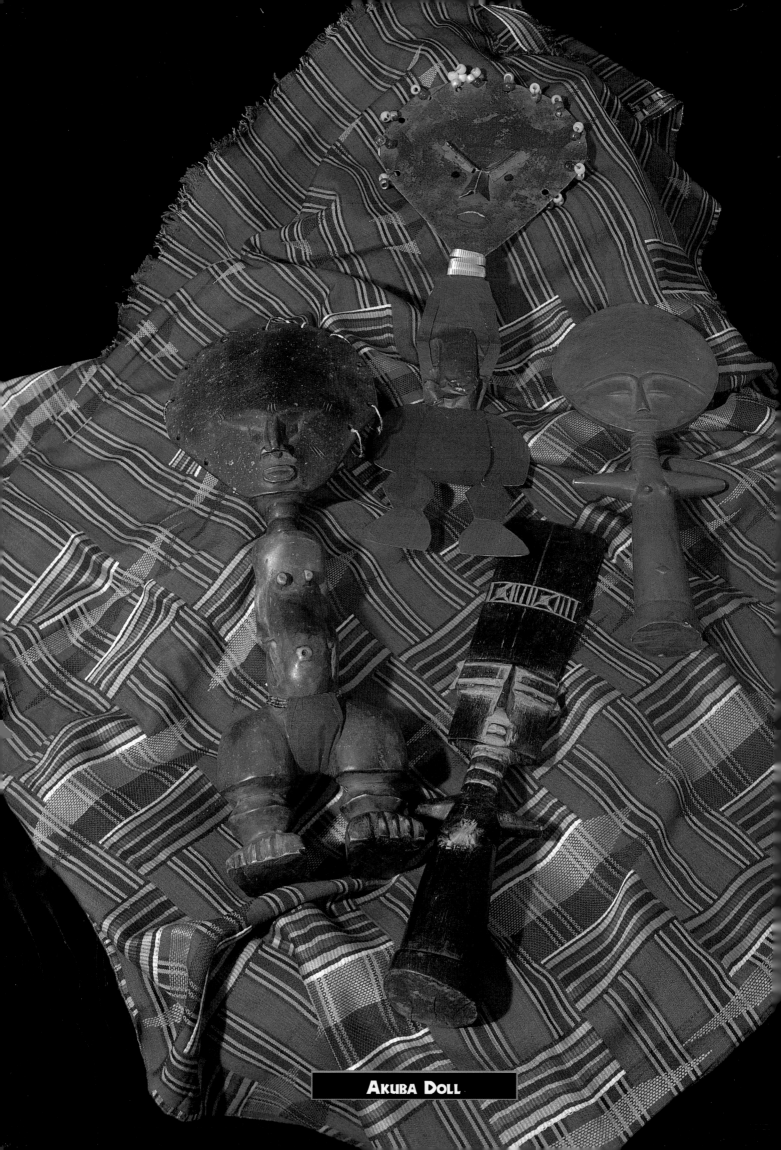

AKUBA DOLL

AKUBA DOLL

Materials: Heavy cardboard such as railroad board in brown or rust, brown paint, brush and sponges, beads, needle and thread, hole punch, scissors, glue, brightly colored fabric, gold ribbon or cording, facial tissue, masking tape.

1. Cut the doll after drawing the shape on a folded piece of paper. The doll can be any size between 10"x 15". Place the cutout pattern on top of your brown cardboard. Trace around the shape with a pencil. Cut out the cardboard doll. Cut a 10" x 1" strip that will be glued to the doll back to make it strong. Carefully separate the arms from the body with scissors.

2. You may choose to make the simple-bodied Akuba doll or the doll wearing the red "diaper". For this doll you must build up the stomach section by making soft balls of facial tissue and placing them together. Tape them in place with several strips of masking tape so the tissue is completely covered. Make sure there are no hard edges with the tape.

3. Paint the raised stomach with a brush and matching paint. Sponge paint all over the doll with a damp sponge section dipped in the paint used for the stomach. Give your doll heavy red lips and black dots for eyes.

4. Make the heavy brow and nose by cutting a piece from the brown cardboard. Fold and slot the nose and brows carefully. This is the hardest part of making the doll.

5. Punch holes around the head. Using a needle and double thread, string four beads per hole. Wrap the gold cord around the doll's throat and glue on the cloth diaper. It can be any color.

The Akuba doll figure is especially a part of the Ashanti people's tradition. Pregnant women tuck the lightweight figure into a belt, headpiece, or bag as an omen for good luck with the new infant...especially that it will be healthy and beautiful. Similar forms are found in other places in Africa representing the same beliefs, but none are as stylized and consistent as the Akuba doll.

THREE AFRICAN FABRICS

THREE AFRICAN FABRICS

Materials for Adinkra Cloth from Ghana: light-colored prewashed cotton, Foamie®, cardboard scraps, black, blue, purple paint, paintbrush, red, green, black embroidery floss, needle, scissors.

MUD CLOTH

1. Tear or cut cloth into strips 8" wide.

2. Make Adinkra stamps by cutting out Foamie in traditional or personal designs as seen on pages 82 and 83. Mount Foamie stamps onto cardboard handles (see Senufo prints handle description, page 16).

3. Divide cloth strips into 8" squares by dipping the edge of a piece of cardboard into paint and stamping it as a divider for each square (see photograph). Fill each square with a stamped pattern repeated in whatever design you wish.

4. Join the decorated strips with simple, colorful embroidery stitches using double floss with knotted ends.

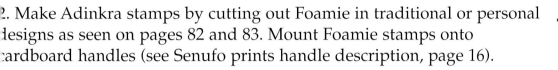

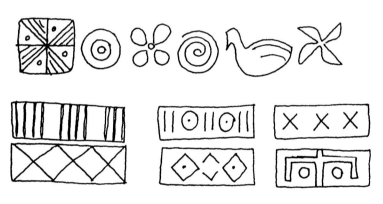

ADINKRA

Materials for faux Adire Eleko and Mali Mud Cloth: White, prewashed cotton fabric no smaller than 15" x 15", black and deep blue acrylic paint, brushes, water, flour, alum (from the spice section), a squeeze bottle with a narrow spout, pencil, spatula for scraping away dried glue, sudsy water for washing the cloth.

1. The prewashed fabric is your "canvas" for creating a traditional African fabric. Look at the design ideas that are usually used for this fabric.

2. Mix the "glue" that will create this design: **Paste Recipe: mix in a blender or a bowl 1/2 cup water, 2 teaspoons of alum, 1/2 cup flour.** After you have blended this pour it into your squeeze bottle. Shake it hard each time you use it. Carefully squirt some onto a practice paper. Is it too thick? Add some water. Too thin? Add some flour. Watch for lumps.

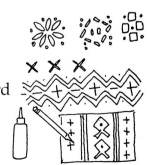

3. Draw with the paste, following the pencil lines on your fabric. When you have finished let it dry.

(continued on page 82)

ADIRE ELEKO

TALL BOBO DANCE MASK

TALL BOBO DANCE MASK

Materials: Any cardboard 28" long and 6-8" wide. A ruler, stapler, scissors, pencil and newspaper for cutting the pattern. Paint or markers: black, brown, yellow, white or beige. The mask can be any combinations of these colors with black dominant. A 28" piece of cardboard for a brace.

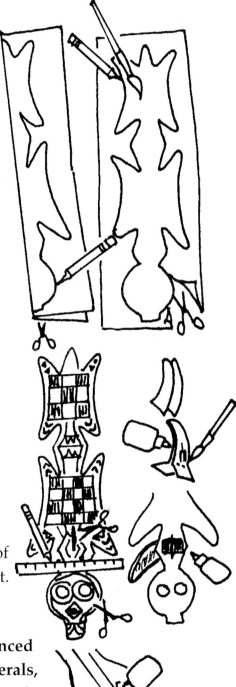

1. These tall masks were carved from lightweight wood. The designs were all different but always had a lot of pattern using checkerboards and triangles.

2. Fold a 28" piece of newspaper and sketch half of the mask. Cut through the second layer following the pencil pattern. Next lay the newspaper pattern on the cardboard that is to be the Bobo mask. Trace around the pattern and cut out the cardboard.

3. Paint the overall mask with a whitish color.

4. Pencil the design onto the painted cardboard. Use a ruler and circle shapes to achieve a symmetrical mask. Apply the color to the mask. Cut out the eyeholes for when it is worn.

5. Make the downturned horn from two cut pieces of cardboard scraps. Paint them a dark color. When they have dried glue them together except for 3/4" at the bottom. Make a single vertical slot in the mask section and glue the horn on. Separate the bottom ends to create tabs that fit through the slot. Glue them to the back of the mask.

6. Prepare a long narrow piece of cardboard. Glue it to the spine of the mask so it has support and will not fall over when you wear it. Attach a 5" crown that fits your head by stapling it to the mask.

These tall masks of the Bobo were worn by young men who danced together after the sowing of crops. Other tribal rituals were funerals, or anytime it was suspected that evil spirits were about. They are also worn at the time of fruit ripening on the bush. Though fruit gathering is no longer important to the Bobo, this traditional harvest ceremony is still performed.
The carved masks must have been a challenge to balance with their great height and awkward shape. The downturned horn is almost always on the Bobo mask. It is meant to "spear" bad spirits.

FLAGS OF THE FANTÉ WARRIORS

FLAGS OF THE FANTÉ WARRIORS

Materials: Colored paper (8 1/2" x 11") or colored fabric, colorful felt, scissors, glue for fabric, pencil and paper for design ideas, a dowel or bamboo skewer for handle, markers or crayons.

. The flag design can be about the designer's interests or something related to a subject being studied. The common elements in each flag are:

- brilliant colors that contrast with each other
- a geometric border of cutout shapes in contrasting colors
- a flag in the left-hand corner: an original design or an existing patriotic flag
- flags can be any size but should be rectangular in shape.

. Using paper and pencil, design the flag. The figures are fanciful. They should be recognizable but abstractions and simplifications of the real thing. Here are some ideas from Fanté flags: More flag ideas on page 83.

| tree | bird | animal | person | town | boat |

. Cut out the fabric rectangle (ours is 12" x 18") or use a piece of colored paper. Cut out the flag, figures, and border pieces from the design. Add color and detail with fabric paints or markers.

. Glue everything in place. Glue or stitch your flag handle in place.

The flags of the Asafo, the warrior people of the Fanté of Ghana, are among Africa's most interesting textiles. The flags adorn villages and towns at festivals and funerals. Often they are carried in dances or displayed as banners. They may depict a story from history. These appliqued patchwork and embroidered flags were inspired by the pageantry, royal arms, and military trappings of the many Europeans who influenced the region from 1471 to 1957, the year of Ghanian independence. Ivory, gold, and slaves were traded by the British, Portuguese, Dutch, French, Swedes, and Danes for 350 years. They were called "Oburinifo" (the people from the hole-in-the-seas horizon). The flags' flamboyant colors and simple forms convey a pride mixed with the tradition of Fanté' imagery.

CENTRAL AFRICA

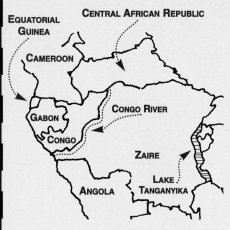

When Europeans penetrated beyond the African coasts they were amazed to find many sophisticated and affluent kingdoms where skilled craftspeople were producing original and creative objects. The forests and wooded savannahs of Equatorial Africa continue to be rich in art traditions such as masks, carved ivory, costumes for rituals, cast bronze figures, and gold and glass beads. Trade from west to east stimulated and contributed to this rich diversity.

THE MANGBETU PEOPLE, distinguished by the elaborate hairstyles worn by the women, are known for their carved ivory, made first from elephant tusks and later warthog tusks and hippopotamus teeth.

Pygmies, people small in stature, are quickly disappearing in population but remain scattered throughout Central Africa. They continue to have an influence in music, song, dance, and dramatic storytelling.

Historically, African art objects have been important for initiation rites. In many cultures the young people experience several passages involving seclusion and physical hardship as they learn tribal values. Young women also have ceremonies to celebrate their physical development, birth, and marriage. Ceremonies involve many forms: costumes, body adornment and symbolic jewelry, face and body painting, brilliant masks that are either worn or held in place, dance, rhythm instruments, and song.

Ancestor worship is a repeated element of artistic expression throughout Central Africa. In Madagascar, for example, carved coffins represent the interests or life's work of the deceased. Carved grave staffs tell stories of the loved one's life. The Bakota people create reliquary, or guardian statues which have become popular with contemporary art collectors. These carved figures are frequently placed *not on the burial site* but at a special place to remind friends and family of the dead person.

carved coffins
from Madagascar

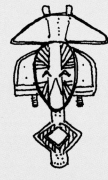

Bakota funeral figure

grave staffs

Kuba mask

EAST AFRICA

The most important sections of East Africa's geography are the extensive coastal ports which have been trading centers for hundreds of years. Ports such as Zanzibar and Mombasa were Africa's gateways to China, India, and Arab lands. Today much of the area is engaged in cattle herding and mixed farming. East Africa provides the world's earliest indications of human activity and handmade tools. Extensive archeological research takes place in the Rift Valley which runs from the Olduvai Gorge in Tanzania to Lake Turkana in Kenya. This region is also known as "safari" country with popular tourism experiencing "the Serengeti" and the abundance of exotic animals in preserves.

AKSUN, an early Christian center in northern Ethiopia, is evidence that representatives of the new faith proselytized into northern and East Africa and established Christian strongholds by the first century A.D. Coptic crosses, unique to early Christianity, are found in this region as well as the enormous stone stelae, which recorded the history of the region. The Aksun stela, at 24 feet, is the tallest in the world. Local tradition claims that the Ark of the Covenant was brought to Aksun by Menelek, the son of Sheba and Solomon, where it is supposed to remain in a carefully guarded building.

SWAHILI CULTURE evolved from extensive overland trading, east to west, spreading the Islam religion. By the 8th Century mosques were constructed and many Africans were Moslems.

Today, art in East Africa is thriving with the **KAMBA** in Kenya who make fine stools, baskets, incised calabashes, jewelry, and forged iron implements. These are made for collectors and for daily use by Africans. The **KISII** are best known for their carved soapstone figurines and utensils. The **MAKONDE** in southern Tanzania have been carving wood for generations. A local legend tells of the first tribesman, a woodcarver, who carved his mate from a log.

Ethiopian woven
containers

Kamba fine jewelry

Kisii soastone
carving

A carved
Makonde figure

SCULPTED ANIMALS

SCULPTED ANIMALS

Materials: A small box like a Jell-O container, black, maroon, yellow, brown and gray paint, 1/4 cup Cheerios®, gold spray paint, tissue paper for fringe, manila folder, cardboard piece 1" x 9", 12" pipe cleaner, paper towel tube, 3 1/2" x 4 1/2" cardboard piece, masking tape, glue, scissors, brushes. (Patterns on page 81.)

Hyena

1. For the body of the hyena cut a slit down the back of your box and wrap masking tape around it to form this shape. Make a hole in the front end for the long triangular-shaped snout. Fold a 2" cardboard piece and stick it into the box hole. Add a 1" tail.

2. Paint the snout and box black. Add white dots of paint. Add maroon dots in the center.

3. Roll four cardboard pieces 1 1/2" long around a pencil and glue them to form tubes. Make four holes in the box bottom and glue in the tubes for the legs. Cut several layers of beige tissue paper 2" long. Lay the paper and cut fringe, leaving a 1/2" top for gluing. Glue the fringe around the entire body of the hyena.

Benin Leopard

1. Cut out two parts of the leopard pattern on page 81. Paint or marker the pieces yellow with brown leopard spots. Make the eyes and mouth. Spray Cheerios with gold paint and glue them onto both sides of the leopard.

2. Make a triangular wedge 4" x 1 3/4". Staple or glue it. Glue the wedge under the body, squeezing the sides together.

Wildebeest

1. Cut out the wildebeest pattern (p. 81) and trace onto a paper tube. Cut around the head, neck, and tail only. Leave the tube body uncut. Trace front and back leg patterns onto 3 1/2" x 4 1/2" cardboard.

2. Make horns by bending 12" pipe cleaner in half, shaping and taping together. With scissors make a small opening between ears and wedge middle of horns into the holes. Tape from underneath. Tape neck and sides together. Tape neck down to neck tab.

3. Cut leg slots about 3/4" from front and back of the tube body. Slot in legs with long ones in front. Paint body gray. Add brown stripes to shoulders and glue on yarn mane, tail, and beard.

KUBA BEADED MASK

KUBA BEADED MASK

Materials: Railroad board 14" x 10", black, green, brown, ochre, white, blue paint, potato or carrot for printing, brush, 1/4 cup puffed wheat cereal, scissors, glue.

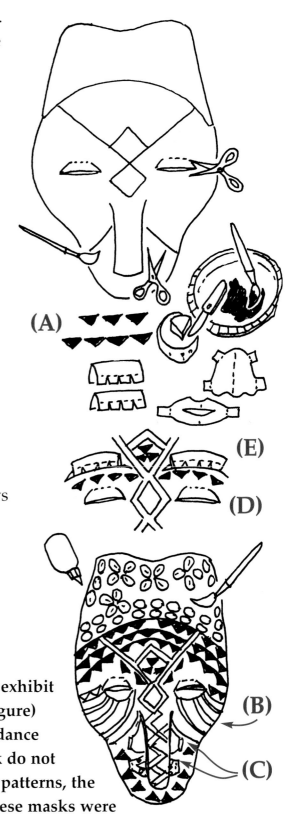

1. Cut out the mask face following the pattern on page 77. Divide the face into sections that will involve printing the diamond design. Mark the eyes and nose strip as they will be partially cut from the mask.

2. Put the black paint on a pie plate. Cut a triangle shape from a carrot or potato or use the foam printing material. Brush paint onto the triangle or dip into the paint. Try your print on a practice sheet of paper. When the triangle is making a strong mark, start printing your rows onto the mask (A).

3. Paint the tear lines in black, white, and ochre onto the mask with a brush (B).

4. Cut out the nose and lips and paint them brown. Carefully cut the nose strip. Glue the nose and mouth pieces onto the mask and under the strip (C).

5. Carefully cut the eyelids halfway up each side but be sure they are uncut at the top (D). Make blue eyebrows and notch them into the mask above the eyes (E).

6. Paint the hat blue. Glue the puffed wheat cereal to look like a cowrie shell design.

The Kuba in Zaire have a strong design talent that they exhibit in their theatrical masks and textiles. *Woot* (an Adam figure) has a sister called *ngady amwaash* (an Eve figure). The dance steps are stylized and feminine. The motifs on the mask do not vary: tears coming from the eyes, the distinct triangular patterns, the cowrie shell hat, and forehead markings. Sometimes these masks were not beaded but rather carved in wood.

KIKUYU INITIATION SHIELDS

KIKUYU INITIATION SHIELDS

Materials: As large a piece of cardboard as possible (both shields are at least 15" tall and 12" wide), brown, black and red paint, potato for printing, paint tray, brush, knife for cutting potato print, pencil and ruler.

1. Take a piece of newspaper with a fold and draw your half-shield on the fold. Cut out the shield following the pencil line. Open it up and see if it is the shape you like.

2. Using the newspaper pattern trace around the cardboard for your shield. Cut it out with strong scissors and carefully use an exacto blade on a carefully protected surface to make the eye.

3. Draw the design onto the cut-out shield. Rub diluted brown paint onto the surface with a paper towel or rag.

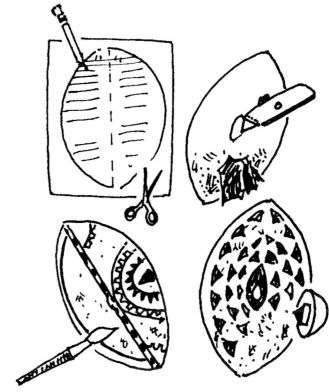

Painted shield

Paint any design you want to have as your own personal "motif" but you must use the red and black colors and put the line down the middle. Also, be sure to cut out the "eye" in the center.

Printed shield

Cut your design from the halved potato center. African designers liked diamonds and triangles. Start printing around the outside edge and work your way inside following the circular design. Cut out the "eye" in the center.

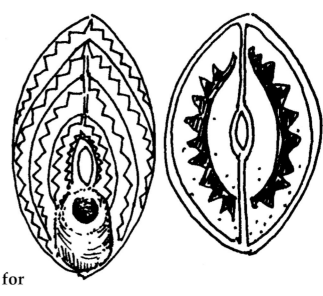

These initiation shields were carved from wood and then painted. War shields were always made of animal hides. The *Kikuyu* initiation in Kenya has been a spur for artistic activity. Each ceremony for boys entering the social status of "warrior" had a "theme" that was to be painted on the shields. Old designs were removed and the boy applied the new ones. Older boys passed on the shields to younger boys. Common to all is the cut out "eye" in the center.

AFRICAN JEWELRY

AFRICAN JEWELRY

Materials: Railroad board, colorful markers, tube pasta, red and black licorice, gold and red paint, plain paper, Cheerios®, carrots, beets, etc., needle, thread, dental floss or heavy thread, yellow, orange and brown paint, salt dough recipe.

Collar necklace (Yoruba)

1. Cut a round railroad board circle. Using a ruler and pencil mark a grid on 2" of the outer edge of the color. Color in the grid with marker.
2. Spray paint the gold pasta, paint the red pasta, cut the red and black licorice into pieces. Make 20 strings of varying lengths stringing pasta, licorice pieces, etc. Attach them every inch to the collar. Glue the pasta pieces to the collar.

Faux amber necklace

1. Make the cooked salt dough recipe*. Roll round balls the size of your choice. Stick a nail or toothpick through the balls and let them dry for 24-36 hours.
2. Paint each ball a yellow color. Let the paint dry. String the balls with pasta or a Cheerios divider and a heavy string.
3. Make rolled tube beads with leftover dough. Insert a toothpick for drying. Paint colorful designs to resemble trade beads.

Funky paper rolls necklace

1. Cut 1"-2" strips of paper 6" long. Make animal patterns on the strips with markers or crayons. Roll the strips and glue the edges. String the "beads" with cut-up carrots, beets, Cheerios, licorice pieces or small pasta.
2. String the necklace parts with dental floss (the best choice) or heavy thread. The vegie parts will shrink. Hang the necklace for drying and after a week push the parts together. It might be a few inches shorter.

Ornaments that are worn in most African cultures symbolize status: married, single, widowed. Many pieces are made of gold, rare shells, or remarkable beads and convey the level of wealth of the person or the relative. Jewelry often conveys tribe or region. Choosing projects that represent "the adorned Africa" was a challenge because all of Africa is decorative.

*Recipe for salt dough: 1 cup salt, 2 cups flour, 4 t. cream of tartar, 2 cups **cold** water. Mix all dry ingredients in a cooking pot. Stir in the cold water, mixing with your hands. Cook on medium heat, stirring constantly, until dough looks like mashed potaotes or a firm ball.*

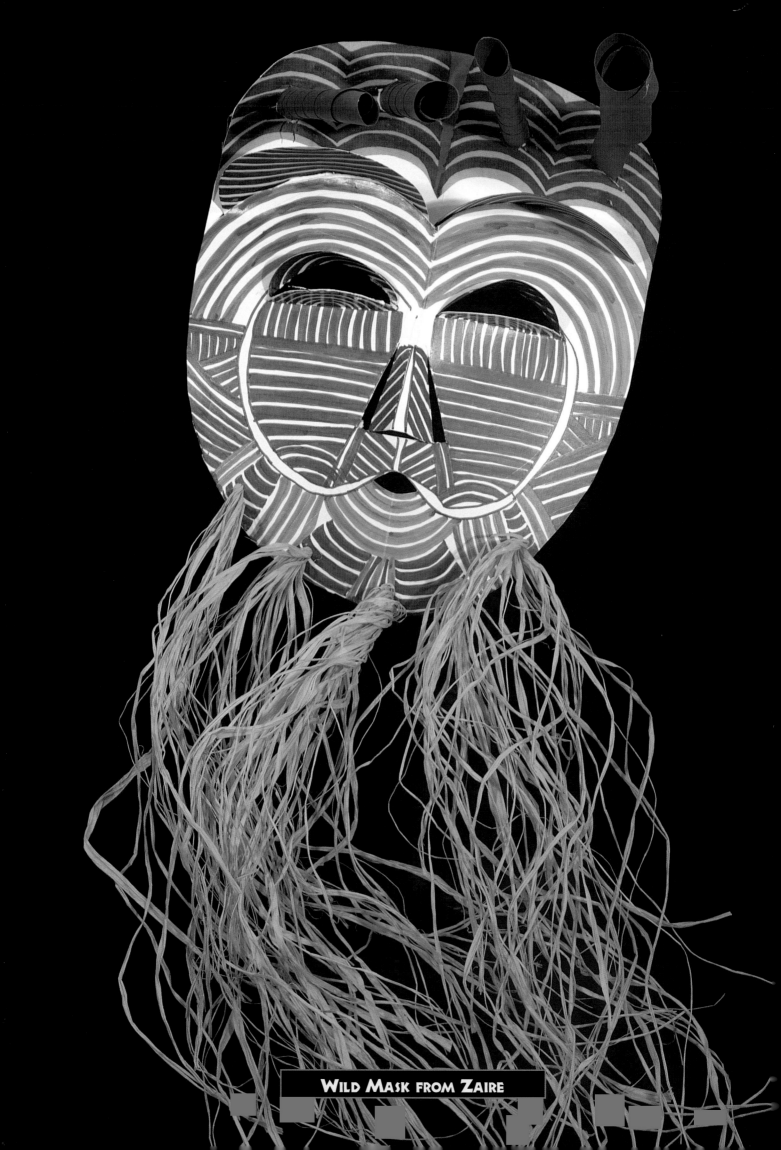

WILD MASK FROM ZAIRE

A WILD MASK FROM ZAIRE

Materials: Manila file cardboard, 40 strands of 24" raffia, black and brown markers, ruler, glue, scissors, hole punch, brown construction paper, exacto point (to be used with adult help), pattern on page 77 which should be enlarged.

1. Draw an outline of the enlarged pattern onto the cardboard. Cut out the notched nose, mouth, eyebrows, and eyelids and mark the eye place.

2. Use your ruler and divide up the surface of the face. You will be drawing curved lines in black or brown marker, as though you were carving a wooden mask. There is no right or wrong design...**but the entire** surface must be covered with line patterns and they must be symmetrical.

3. When you have made patterns on all the parts (the front and back of the eyebrows, eyelids, and eyes), cut the notches and insert them into their cut line (a), (b), (c). Be patient as this takes effort. When they are in place, glue them.

4. Try on the mask. Cut out the half-circle eyes so you can see. Hole punch where the raffia is inserted. Make dime-sized holes for the paper horns on the forehead. Take a tuft of two or three raffia strings, fold them in half, and stuff the fold into one of the holes at the mask bottom. You should have at least ten raffia stuffings.

The horns
Cut four strips of brown construction paper 3" x 12". Wrap them around a straight pencil. Unravel the coil and pull it. Insert each end into the dime-sized hole as though they were horns. Glue them in the hole on the back of the mask. Punch a hole on each side and try on your mask.

This handsome mask is traced to the Songye in Zaire. It was worn for an initiation ceremony. There are several variations of this mask with the distinctive line patterns and the forehead horns.

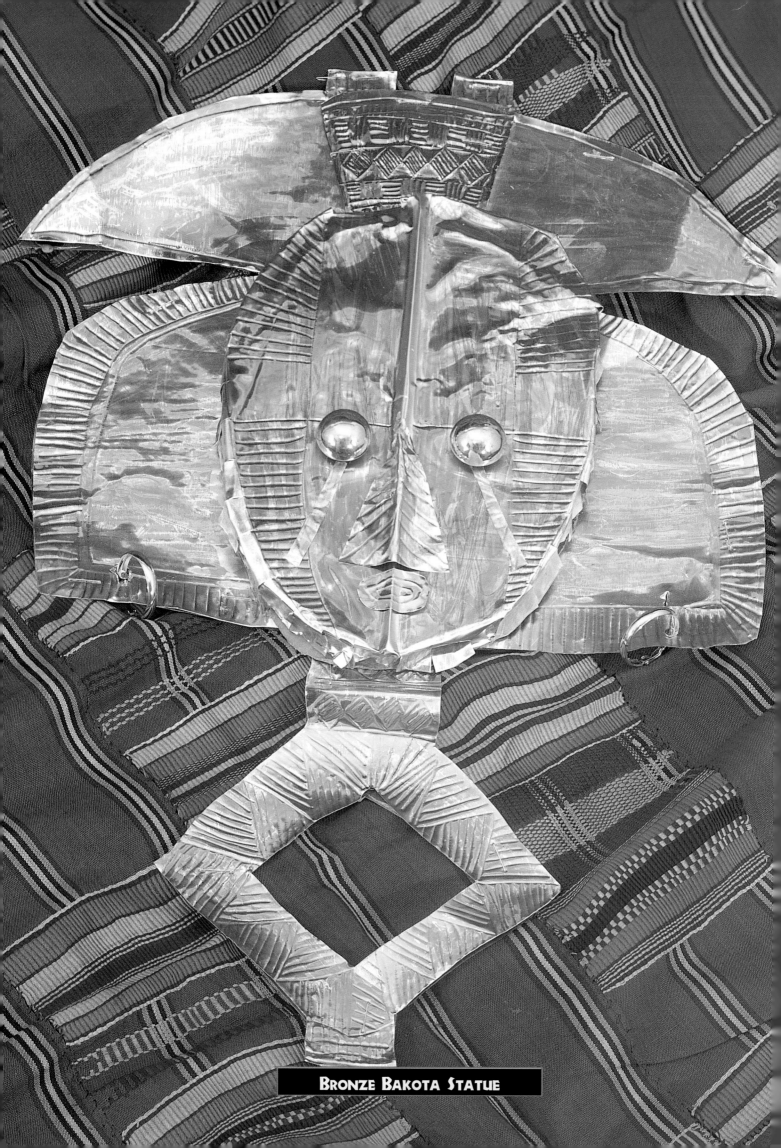

BRONZE BAKOTA STATUE

BRONZE BAKOTA STATUE

Materials: A piece of railroad board (20" x 18"), an aluminum baking sheet 20" wide, stapler, scissors, dull pencil, toothpick or nail tip, permanent gold or orange markers, two gold buttons for eyes, gold rings for earrings, glue, newspaper and 1/2" thick piece of cardboard.

1. The funeral sculpture piece is symmetrical. Enlarge the pattern and trace it on a fold of newspaper. There are three parts: (A) the top with a center shield, (B) the wing-like piece the head rests on, and (C) the diamond base. These are all traditional and are not altered in their basic shape. You should include them in a single pattern piece.

2. Now trace the newspaper pattern on the cardboard. Cut a single piece from the cardboard, saving the paper pattern. Lay the pattern on an aluminum sheet. Trace around the pattern onto the aluminum.

3. Cut the the single piece of aluminum sheet. Color it with the marker to look gold. Make an orange border around the edge of the top section. With the tip of a tool scratch designs around the shapes. Any design form is appropriate. This technique is called repousse'.

4. Glue the heavy cardboard oval on the second section. Cut out the oval face to fit the cardboard shape, allowing an extra inch around the entire face for cut tabs. Color the oval with orange marker. Scratch in your repousse' designs.

5. Add the eyes, nose, and mouth. Pay close attention to their placement (the bottom half of the oval face). Clip in earrings or brass metal rings. Staple around the edges of the sculpture to bond the cardboard and foil.

These bronze statues are called "reliquary figures". They are made by the Bakota and Fang of Gabon. They stand above the barkcloth receptacles holding the bones of ancestors. They are guardians of the bones...not images of the dead person. They are meant to ward off evil which might desecrate the ancestral remains. The metal acts like a mirror and is believed to reflect back any evil that threatens.

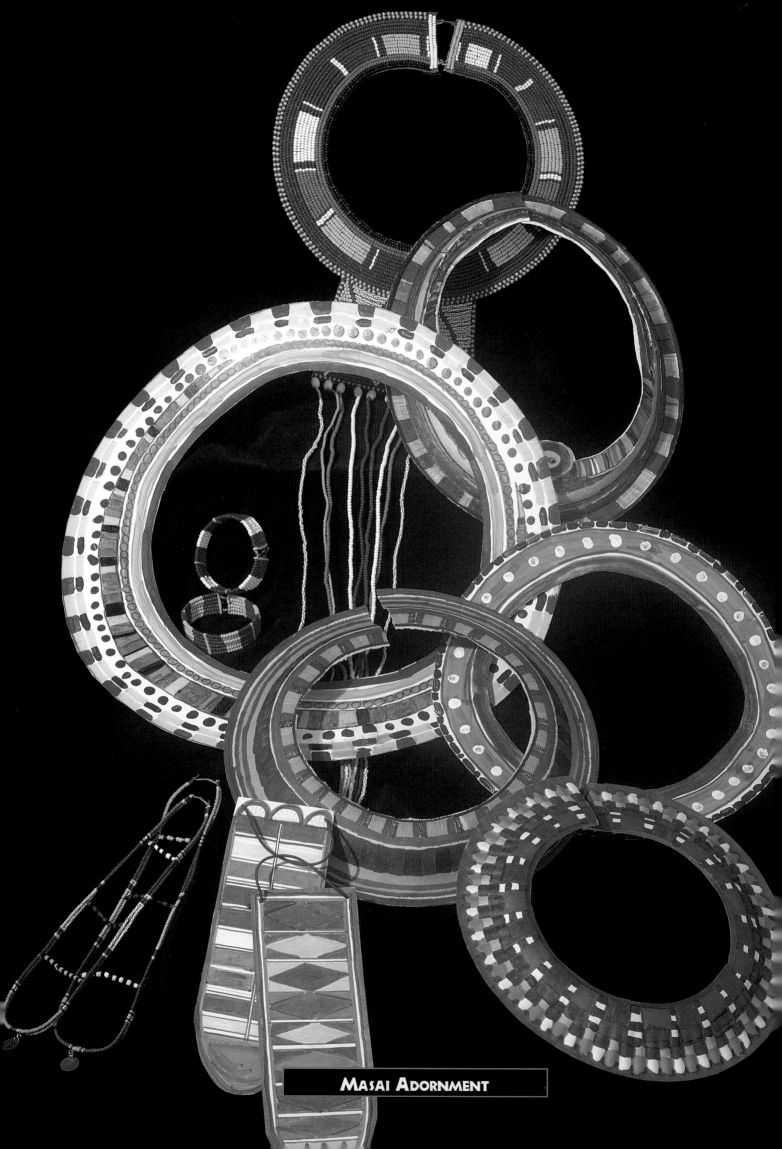

MASAI ADORNMENT

MASAI ADORNMENT

Materials: Any plain white paper plate with a rim, 5" x 6" white railroad board, red, blue, yellow, green, and black colored markers, scissors, a pencil, an exacto knife (use with adult help), string or elastic.

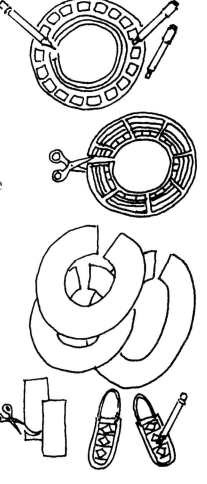

Beaded collars

1. Look at the colorful collars in the photograph. Think about your design. Color it on paper. Colors and designs are repeated in rows. The Masai women wear the collars on top of one another. The Masai men wear colorful chokers and beads but not the collars. Both wear elaborate earrings.

2. Choose a paper plate. The designs are on the first 1" to 3" of the paper plate rim. With your pencil sketch the pattern. Choose the marker or crayon colors: red, green, blue, yellow, and black are the colors the Masai use in their beading.

3. Color your collar. When it is finished, cut the back where it is going to slip over the head and rest on the shoulders.

4. Cut out the center with a scissors. Make more than one collar and stack them around your neck as the Masai do. This only works if different sized paper plates and cardboard collar sizes are made.

Masai earrings

1. Cut 5" x 6" cardboard piece in half for two 2 1/2" x 6" pieces. Round the bottom of each piece and decorate with colorful Masai designs.

2. Cut string in half and attach to top of earrings for hanging over each ear.

The Masai, once large landholders, were forced by the British in the late 1800s into southern Tanzania. They continue to live in the traditional way in villages of mud huts surrounded by thornbush fences, which contain their cattle herds at night. The collars worn by Masai women symbolize their status: single, married, etc.

SIMPLE STAFFS AND MASKS

SIMPLE STAFFS AND MASKS

Materials: Double paper plates for masks, buttons, tempera or acrylic paint, scissors, railroad board 24" long, black and brown fine-tipped markers for detailing, wooden yardsticks or dowel pieces to back the staffs.

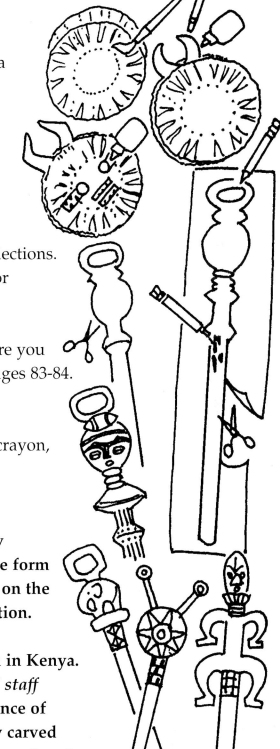

Two simple masks

1. Paint each of the masks any color that is preferred. Ours are replicas of two-horned animal masks. Cut out a pair of horns that are glued at the top. Give the horns color and etched detail.

2. Make small vision holes where the eyes will be. Glue on buttons and paper mouths.

The status staffs

1. These staffs are inspired by chief staffs in museum collections. Staffs have three parts: (a) the long stick, (b) the animal or power symbol in the middle, (c) sometimes a handle.

2. Decide the figure for the staff. Cut it out of paper before you trace it on the cardboard. Look at the pattern ideas on pages 83-84. Add as much pattern to the staff parts as you wish.

3. Color the figure with a combination of paint, marker, crayon, and oil pastels.

These masks are made for the *Goli* dance performed by the Baule people on the Ivory Coast. The repeated circle form in the eyes, the dots between the eyes, and the designs on the horn all have secret meaning to this traditional celebration.

The *Akuba* figure is from a staff carved by the Akamba in Kenya. The *elephant staff* is carved by the Ashanti. The *horned staff* was made for a Zulu chief and emphasizes the importance of cattle in their economy. The *human figure* was probably carved by the Tsonga and is wearing a Tsongan helmet and leg and neck rings. The Tsonga and Zulu traded goods, and the staffs were power symbols.

CAMEROON BEADED BEAUTIES

CAMEROON BEADED BEAUTIES

Materials: Railroad board 22" long and 4"-6" high for each hat. Additional pieces 8"x 8" square. Lizard pieces can be manila folder scraps, etc., 12" long and 4" wide. Markers should be bright primary colors. Pencil, ruler, scissors, stapler, graph paper and glue.

Beaded hatband

Measure the wearer's head. A band of paper 22"-24" long will fit most foreheads. Make a design on graph paper. Dab with marker colors on the pencilled shapes. Transfer the pattern to the hatband and color. Very little white paper should show. Adjust the hatband and securely tape the ends.

Hat with a crown

Lay the hatband on a piece of paper with the open end down. Trace around the band, making a circle. It will probably be 7"-9" across. Add an extra 2" to the edge. Pencil in your design for the crown and color it in. Cut 1" notches around the outside edge of the crown. Fit it inside the hatband and glue.

Hat with face or dangling creature

1. This hat has a stylized face at the center. Think about the face and draw a few ideas. Perhaps it is your face or a friend's. Keep it a secret and let people guess when the hat is modelled.

2. Follow the instructions for a beaded hatband. Leave a 5" square empty. Cut graph paper that is 5" x 5". Design the face and color it. Be inventive and add 3-D features. Glue it to the hat front.

3. Choose a special animal or symbolic shape. Draw it and color your drawing. Cut 1" x 18" strips. Glue two strips so they cross at the center. Fold the third strip in half and glue all securely to the hatband. Attach the dangling form at the top.

Lizard from Cameroon

1. Fold a 12" x 6" paper and cut out the lizard pattern. Enlarge or reduce your lizard on the copy machine.

2. Using the patterns from pages on 83 to 84 or those on the samples, decorate your lizard as though it were beaded. Watch carefully for: • symmetry • dividing up the body lengthwise and crosswise • covering the entire surface with color.
Have fun! These lizards are meant to be beautiful.

Beautiful beadwork on clothing, utensils, and masks is common in Cameroon. An appropriate African tale by Baba Wague Diakite' is *The Hatseller and the Monkeys*, Scholastic Press, N.Y., 1999.

FOREHEAD MASK FROM ZAIRE

FOREHEAD MASK FROM ZAIRE

Materials: Cardboard 20" x 10" , masking tape, scissors, black, brown, green acrylic or tempera paint and brushes, pencil, newspaper, 1" tube for mouth.

. Place a folded newspaper on a surface. Draw half of the mask on it. The length is 10" and the width is 10". Remember the ears are part of the main mask piece.

. After you have cut out your half-mask, open the pattern on the fold and make alterations. It should be symmetrical. Trace around it onto the cardboard and cut out your mask.

. Make the protruding brows by cutting your newspaper pattern in half, removing the ears. Trace onto remaining cardboard. Draw 1" tabs on top center, sides and bottom sides (a). Snip 1" deep into center and sides and fold slotted pieces under (b). Cut out brow piece.

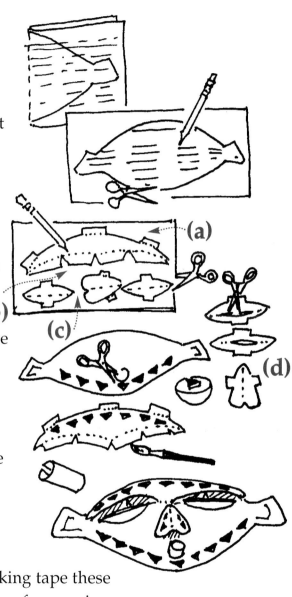

. On remaining cardboard draw the 6" eyes and 4" nose shape (c). Draw two tabs on each. Cut out features. Fold each in middle. Make a cut in center of each eye fold.

. Paint all the parts of the mask. We have used a simple triangle potato print to decorate the edge with black triangles. Cut slots and insert the tabs of the eyes and the nose.

. Make the tube mouth hole and insert the mouth, masking tape these relief pieces on the back. Cut a hole on each side for string for wearing the mask. These masks were worn on the forehead. When the ceremony was complete they hung over the wall above the door.

These masks from Zaire were worn by men in the Pende tribes for theatrical purposes. The men were masquerading as women. The masks always represented a stereotype of women: the proud beauty, the temptress, the chief's wife. Often a prostitute was the favorite image depicted by a pursed mouth, downcast slotted eyes, and mincing flirtatious dance steps. They were called *kanene (kuh nee nee).*

THE TALKING DRUM

ART MUSIC MATH LITERACY
THE TALKING DRUM

Materials: Two same-sized cups, masking tape, a big brad, heavy string or hemp cord, a big-eyed needle, glue, brown shoe polish or paint for rubbing on the drum. For the rattles: a tomato sauce can, masking tape, brown, white, black paint, brush, 1/4" stick. For the pod rattle: 10 very small paper cups, brown string, needle, stick, markers and beans.

Talking drum

1. Punch a small slit in the bottom of each cup. Put the bottoms together and insert a brad through both cup bottoms. Spread the flanges to attach the cups. You have an hourglass shape that is the same as that of a carved wooden talking drum.

2. Cover the cups with strips of masking tape. Tape over the cup openings making at least two layers. Either paint the tape or rub on brown shoe polish with a tissue.

3. Wrap hemp rope, raffia, or heavy twine around the drum ends, making at least five layers, and gluing as you wrap. Lightly tape masking tape around the glued rope and let dry for several hours, keeping the rope in place while it dries. Use a large-eyed needle strung with ten feet of rope (wrapped in a ball for easy handling) and catch it in each end of the drum going back and forth until you have surrounded the drum with a rope web. This is difficult and will take patience. Tuck your drum under your arm and play it with your palm.

Drum rattle

1. Tape over the opening of a tomato-sauce size can after placing 20 beans or rocks in the can cavity. Put masking tape on the entire can. Punch a hole in the side of the can and insert a 1/4" dowel or stick. Paint the stick drum with African designs.

"Pod" rattle

1. The pod shaker in the picture is an important sound in African rhythm. Think about what you could use as a substitute for pods: small paper or plastic cups would work. Put some beans in each cup and tape the tops securely. Design each cup using ideas from the pattern pages. Gather the cups together by stringing with a big-eyed needle and some dental floss or strong thread. Put the needle through each cup bottom. Wrap the loose thread ends with yarn at the shaker end of a strong stick.

The Yoruba Talking Drum is called the dundun (doon doon). It makes voicelike sounds.

A recommended African story is by Angela Shelf Medearis and Terea Shaffer, *The Singing Man,* Holiday House, New York, 1994.

SOUTHERN AFRICA

The cinema-influenced image of Africa with broad savannahs, high grassy plains, and snow-covered majestic mountains by wide lakes describes parts of South and East Africa. Both share the reputation of the safari and the animal preserves. And rightly so. The earliest indication of people in the region are the Matopa Hill caves where the Sans Bushmen people left their cave art of animals essential to their survival. Incised ostrich egg flasks have been found in children's burial sites dating back 8,000 years. They emphasize the eland deerlike animal. By 800 A.D. large settlements had emerged and cattle had become a measure of wealth and power. Burial sites from this period contain ivory carvings, beads, and even Chinese celadon ceramics, clues to the extensive trade throughout Africa.

MAPUNGUBWE in eastern Botswana was a trading center in the 1100s. Gold was used as a currency, the first indication of gold "money" in Africa. **GREAT ZIMBABWE** was a trading center for 200 years, with a population of 75,000. A fine stone wall encircled the city. Carved birds on tall staffs welcomed visitors and are the only relics remaining of the legendary city of wealth. The famous conical tower of stone and some walls remain for a visitor's exploration.

The **ZULUS** in eastern South Africa were neighbors to the Xhosa. These neighboring groups were often in conflict over cattle and land boundaries. Shaka, the great Zulu chief in the 19th Century, is credited with the establishment of the carved wooden chief chair as a status symbol. Chairs carved from a single piece of wood became an important power symbol to lesser chiefs in other chiefdoms. Rulers also used headrests, similar to wooden stools, as a sign of power.

carved chief chairs

a carved headrest

staffs of symbolic power

SOUTHERN AFRICA

Th ecology of Southern Africa encompasses six biotic land zones from the northwest desert to the Karoo, a semidesert. The Zulu-natal region is wooded savanna with over 75 species of bats.

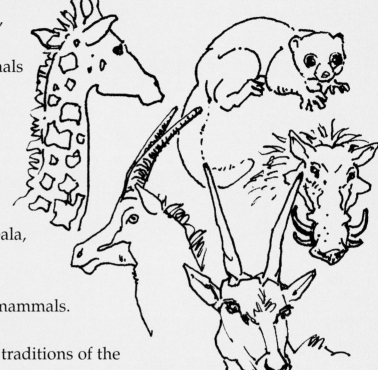

The primates include two species of baboons, the Sandango monkey, and bush babies. Mammals represent most of the African animals we associate with this continent and can be observed in the Krueger Reserve and the Kalahari Gemsbok Park: African elephant (which is bigger than the Indian elephant), rhinoceros, warthog, hippopotamus, zebra, giraffe, cape buffalo, oryx, sable, roan antelopes, wildebeest, springboks, kuda, impala, and eland.

Dolphins and right whales are common sea mammals.

Though their population is small, the artistic traditions of the **NDEBELE** (enn duh bee lee) are astonishing. Their bright geometric designs cover housefronts, aprons, and other objects today with little change from traditional patterns of generations.

The beadwork and elaborate geometric patterns painted on compound walls, almost exclusively by the women, reflect age-old passages of time and status of the wearer. Beaded wrapped cloaks have been replaced with commercial woolen blankets, with a Ndebele touch.

The Zulus produced handsome earplugs for the important ceremony performed on each child. The small hole was plugged with larger and larger plugs. They might be made of ivory or carved horn. The architecture and organization of a Zulu compound impressed the Europeans of the 19th Century.

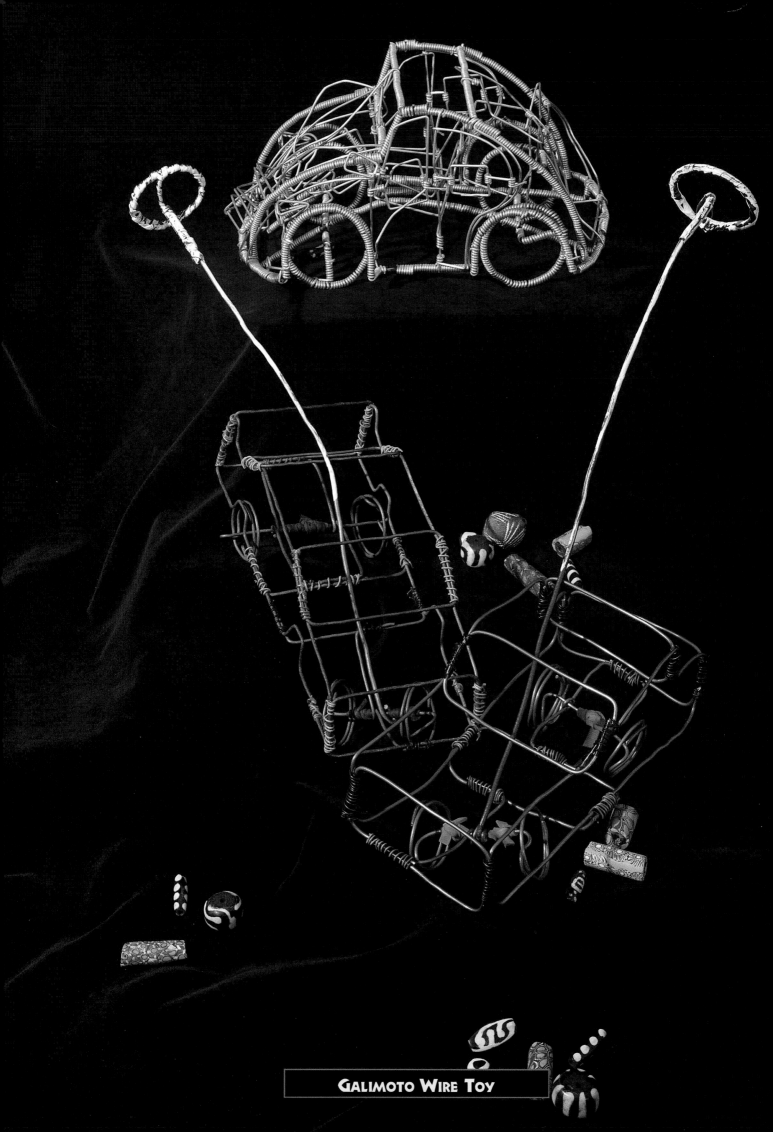

GALIMOTO WIRE TOY

SCULPTURE   ENGINEERING   MATH   LITERACY

A GALIMOTO WIRE TOY

Materials: 5 ft. of copper wire or colorful telephone wire, fine wire for wrapping connecting ends, wire cutters or strong scissors for some wire, needle-nosed pliers, 2 wooden blocks the size of the toy, hammer, three medium-sized rubber bands, electrical tape.

1. Nail wooden blocks together to make a form for your toy.

2. Wrap approximately 2 ft. of wire around the length of the blocks using needle-nosed pliers to force the wire into shape. Make two sides (A).

3. Wrap about 14" of wire around the front of the block for windshields, bumpers, etc. Make five rectangles (B).

4. Cut seven pieces of 1/2" electrical tape and wrap joinings of the two sides of each rectangle (C).

5. Cut ten pieces of 1" electrical tape. Tape windshields, bumpers, and bottom chassis to sides.

6. Cut 10 pieces of 8" wrapping wire and securely wrap all taped joinings of your toy.

7. For wheels cut two pieces of 2 ft. wire. Find a cylinder 1 1/2" in diameter. We used a chair leg. Wrap the wire around several times. Save straight wire in the center for an axle and wrap the other wheel. Total length of your wheels and axle should measure 2 1/2". Make two sets (D).

8. Cut an 8 1/2" piece of wire for the back wheel chassis. Make a rectangle (like windshields) that reaches from the bottom to the back bumper to center section and wraps around the back axle between them. Tape the joinings (E).

9. Cut a 5" piece of wire for the front wheel chassis. Wrap the middle of the wire around the front axle and bend ends so they fit between center section and bottom of front bumper. Cut a 26" piece of copper wire for steering wheel. Bend bottom end firmly around the axle. Bend top end to form steering wheel circle about 2" in diameter (F, G).

10. Tape front and back wheel chassis in place with 6 pieces of 1 /2" electrical tape. Tape steering wheel. Tie one rubber band around back axle and one on either side of the front axle. The steering column and chassis wires will be between.

11. Cut six pieces of 8" wrapping wire. Securely wrap all taped front and back wheel chassis parts to complete your galimoto.

Wheeled toys made of wire with amazing engineering and design techniques are common throughout Africa. "Gali" means wire and "moto" means wheels.

An appropriate African story by Karen Lynn Williams, ***Galimoto***, *Lothrop, Lee and Shepard* Books, N.Y., 1990.

ANCIENT ART

ANCIENT ART

Materials: Plastic eggs that separate in the middle, white acrylic or spray paint, brown shoe polish, a fine-tipped, permanent black marker, pencil, spray fixative. For trays collect Foamie@, scissors, pencil, paper, tempera paint, paper for printing, twine, paper for booklet.

The Kalahari ostrich eggs

1. Assemble as many dividing plastic eggs as you need.

2. Cut a 1/4" strip of masking tape and tape it around the separating midsection.

3. Brush paint or spray paint the eggs whitish. Let the eggs dry. Gently dab and rub brown shoe polish on the surface to give the eggs an antique look.

4. Think about the surface of your egg and your design. Lightly pencil in your mathematical spaces before you make your design. Draw the penciled design with black or brown marker. Spray fixative on the finished eggs.

Designs from these ancient eggs:

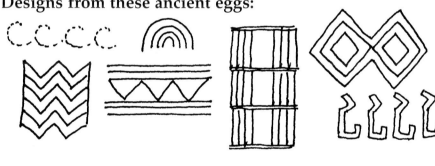

The cave art cover for a booklet

1. Find examples of the remarkable pectoglyphs and cave drawings from 10,000 years ago. The giraffe sample is from Saharan rock art and the figures are from the South Africa Matopa area. Or study the animals and make up your own animal for the cover.

2. Draw your final design on a paper 5"x 7" or whatever size you wish.

3. Using a same size piece of Foamie press the drawn lines onto the sponge, transferring the animal drawing. Lightly paint the cover with paint. Press the print on a practice paper before making your final print. Assemble the booklet.

A male ostrich can be 8 feet tall and weigh 350 pounds. The smaller female ostrich lays eggs that are 5" to 7" big and weigh 3 pounds. The ostrich was valued for its plumage and eggs. One egg could feed eight people. The shells were carved into beads and used for inlays. The large hollow shells were used as water containers. Engraved eggs were found in the graves of children. Decorated eggs were done by the Sans (Bushmen) 10,000 years ago.

CHI WARA

CHI WARA HAT

Materials: Black cardboard, an assortment of large and small shapes, scissors, glue, stapler, tempera paint, raffia or dried grasses, tape.

1. Measure a strip of cardboard 6" thick and long enough to go around the upper part of your head like a crown. Staple or glue it together. It should be at least 6" wide and usually 24" long.

2. Attach a piece of cardboard across the top in one of the ways suggested. Glue. Let the glue dry.

 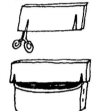  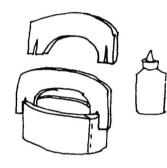

3. With smaller scraps of cardboard add a variety of forms typical of the Chi Wara to your hat. Build it as high as you can. Below are some ideas from Chi Wara hats in museums.

4. Punch holes and add raffia or dried grasses to the base, the back, and along the sides. Tape them down on the inside of your hat.

Chi Wara hats are worn by the Bambara people in the African country of Mali. The symbol represents an antelope—important for its swiftness as game and for its actions which are copied in dance form at the Chi Wara Festival. This festival is about planting and honors seeds, sowing, rain, and all things that produce an abundant crop. All of Africa celebrates planting festivals essential to food production.

TWO MUSICAL INSTRUMENTS

TWO MUSICAL INSTRUMENTS

Materials: For the rattle a forked twig about 1/4" in diameter, railroad board or a manila file folder, brown shoe polish or paint, markers, crayons, stapler, scissors, beans, pebbles or rice for the sound. For the sanza (piano) a flat box about 5"x 7", cardboard scraps, 7-10 craft sticks, glue, brown paint or shoe polish.

"Calabash" rattle

1. Cut a forked stick that is 15" long for the rattle and at least 10" long for the handle. It should be 1/4" in diameter.
2. Using a circle pattern cut 10 duplicate circles from the cardboard. Cut a 2" disc. Color all the edges with African designs with crayons and markers (see pages 82-83). Rub shoe polish or light paint over each disc. You are replicating a calabash which is usually beige in color.
3. Punch a hole exactly in the center of each flat disc. Staple the edges leaving a two-inch gap for stuffing beans, rice, etc. After inserting the beans staple the opening closed.
4. Gently push the discs onto the longest part of the stick. Lastly push the small disc onto the stick which will act as a "stopper". Wrap yarn around the bottom of the stick to keep all circles from falling off. Shake your rattle. How does it sound?

Sanza or thumb piano

1. Tape the lid to the body of a flat box about 5"x 7" big. Cut a semi circle in the bottom third of the box. Using the pattern on page 83 and cardboard scraps cut the two legs, two arms and head. Glue or tape them to the box top. If the surface of the box needs to be covered, masking tape the entire box, giving more strength to the body parts.
2. Paint the box and body part or rub shoe polish onto the surface with a rag or tissue.
3. Line the craft sticks up in pairs. Cut one inch off two end sticks, 3/4" off the next pair, and 1/2" off the next pair and leave one craft stick long. Glue them in symmetrical rows onto the box. Pluck each one to hear the hollow, thumping sound.

The sanza was collected among the Asande who live in Zaire and Sudan. The sanza is not used in an ensemble but is the instrument of the strolling man singing ballads and songs about his personal experience (a griot). Most are simple boxes. Ours is said to represent the ecstacy of an arm-waving dancer. It is thought the sanza is carved by a specific unknown carver because several have been found in the region in this unusual style.

SLOTTED AFRICAN ANIMALS

SLOTTED AFRICAN ANIMALS

Materials: Any type of cardboard that can be cut easily but will hold attached pieces such as railroad board, manila folders. Any art supplies such as paint and brushes, markers, crayons and oil pastels, scissors, pattern pages 78-80.

1. Find the patterns for slotted animals on pages 78-80.
2. Enlarge them using a copy machine.
3. Cut out the animal you like (and its parts) and trace around it on cardboard. You can darken the features on the pattern such as eyes and horns by rubbing the back with your graphite pencil lead and then tracing on the lines, transferring them to the cardboard.

(a) cutting from the pattern page   (b) rubbing on the pattern back   (c) cardboard transfer

  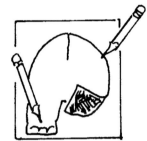 

4. Study pictures of your animal. Notice the different colors on the underbelly, ears, nose, and tail. Color the surface of your animal. Put color on the back and front of each piece. Here are some texture ideas:

crayon covered scratched, then painted over	stippling with paint on a dry toothbrush	sponge on crayon	making spots with paint-dipped pencil eraser	a dry brush dipped in paint

5. Slot the animals together. You can reduce the pattern pieces to make animal babies. Study the colors of the young. They might be very different. Make a diorama by placing savannah animals in that geography, rain forest animals in that geography, etc.

African beads (see photograph on page 36)
While you are applying pattern, texture, and color to your African animals, create some patterned beads using the same techniques:
1. Cut strips of butcher paper 1 1/2" to 2" wide and 12" long.
2. Cover the paper strip with the pattern of one animal.
3. Roll the strip around a pencil and glue the end.
4. String them with such things as cut carrots, soaked beans, small beads, yam or beet squares, etc. Hang them to dry. There will be some shrinkage with drying. Adjust the string for wearing.

Recommended African stories about animals are: Julius Lester and David Shannon, *How Many Spots Does a Leopard Have?* and Verna Aardema and Beatriz Vidal's, *Bringing the Rain to Kapiti Plain*, Dial Books, N.Y., 1981.

TWO CEREMONIAL PUPPETS

TWO CEREMONIAL PUPPETS

Materials: A 12" piece of 1/4" wooden doweling, manila folder scraps, fine-tipped markers, pictures of African ceremonial dress, pattern of puppets, needle and dental floss or 6 brads, glue, scissors, a pencil.

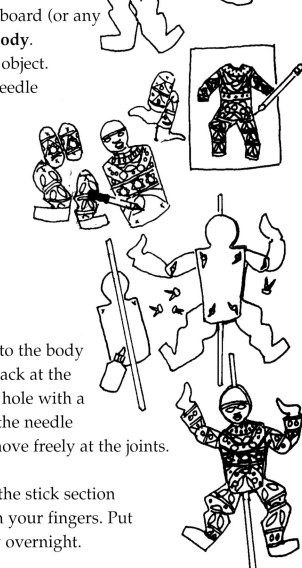

These costumed figures could also be adapted to a full-size costume, worn by a person, or made into oversized puppet figures.

1. Find the puppet pattern pieces on pages 77, 82, and cut them out. Trace around each piece on the manila folder cardboard (or any heavier paper). **Cut a second piece for the head and body.** Carefully pierce the sections marked "X" with a sharp object. There should be 6 punctured holes, big enough for a needle or a brad tip.

2. Draw the costume in pencil on a trial paper using the pattern pieces. Think about the colors. Notice that one puppet is heavily patterned and one is simple. Consider making up a costume of an original design.

3. Apply the pattern to the cardboard pieces with fine-tipped markers.

4. Lay out the pieces to form the figure. Glue the stick to the body back before joining. Let glue dry. Now join front and back at the pierced sections with a needle and floss or pierce each hole with a brad. If using a needle and thread make a knot, bring the needle through, and make a second knot. The parts need to move freely at the joints.

5. Now that all the joints are joined, add some glue to the stick section on both front and back of the puppet. Press down with your fingers. Put some heavy books on each side and let the puppet dry overnight.

6. When the puppet is dry, try it out. Twirl the stick. Your puppet should dance.

The raffia and knitted striped string costumes of the Pende people in Zaire were worn by the instructors who taught Pende boys in an initiation camp. Their identity is secret and only revealed to the boys at the end of the training. Both boys and *minganji* (instructor) return to the camp to dance together. The ritual has a special relationship with the spirits of the dead.

THREE AFRICAN DOLLS

THREE AFRICAN DOLLS

Materials: Black or brown fabric 15" x 15", a small cardboard tube, a 12" cardboard tube, colorful crayons, oil pastels or fine-tipped markers, brown, black and maroon markers or crayons, glue, puffed wheat, 12" x 12" brown paper, buttons, beads, glue, scissors, needle and thread, white paint and paper strips, tape, ruler and pencil, batting.

Tall tube doll (Zaire carved wooden doll)

1. A tall tube such as a paper towel or cut-down mailing tube is good. Measure the tube and cut a brown paper cover to wrap around. Cut two 4" x 2" strips for arms. Cut the hair fringe in a connecting band 20" x 3" long. Cut another band for the bottom 1" long and 12" long.

2. On the flat brown paper use a ruler and pencil to draw a design. Refer to African designs on pattern pages 83,84. Complete the design and glue the paper to the tube, glue on the hair fringe and bottom fringe, glue on puffed wheat (for cowrie shells). Glue rolled arms.

Small tube doll (Ndebele)

1. Cut a piece of white paper the length and width of your tube. Using a pencil and ruler plan the pattern rows. Color the patterns with crayon or fine-tipped markers. Glue the strip to the tube.

2. Cut an 8" circle of black or brown cloth. Make a ball of batting and push it into the circle middle. Sew big stitches around the edge of the cloth circle and gather it tight. This is the doll head. Stuff it into the tube top that has been slathered with glue. With white paint and a fine-tipped brush, paint detail on the head. Cut the white crown out of a folded piece of paper 3" x 3/4". Glue to the head.

Beaded cloth doll (fashioned from a tiny good-luck amulet)

1. Cut a doll from double layers of 12" x 12" black cotton. Sew the random beads and buttons with some being the eyes and the mouth.

2. Sew 1/2" outline stitches with black thread around the entire doll pattern. Double sew the hair tufts. Leave 4" unsewn and stuff with batting. Finish sewing the doll.

As in every culture dolls are made from available materials and are not meant to last beyond the child's need. The adapted tube doll from Zaire is of the early Kuba dynasty.

A NDEBELE HOUSEFRONT

A NDEBELE HOUSEFRONT

Materials: White school paper taped at a seam to create a mural 9 feet x 6 feet, brushes, tempera or acrylic paint colors of choice, pencil, graph paper, ruler, yardsticks, masking tape, wide black marker or black paint and 1/2" brush, water, cleanup materials.

Group mural

1. Find books* that portray the colorful housefronts of the Ndebele (enn duh bee lee) people in Zimbabwe and the Transvaal province of South Africa.
2. Have each group design their housefront and front wall after studying the geometric designs. Using graph paper, pencil, ruler, and crayons or markers, make a symmetrical design, true to the geometric shapes and colors of the Ndebele.
3. Cut the white school paper in two 9-foot strips. Tape them together at the horizontal seam. Turn the taped-together papers over and have the group begin to draw their house design with pencil and yardsticks.
4. The group may wish to also create an Ndebele figure in traditional dress near the house. The women painted the house, usually as brides heralding their own unique pride in color and design.

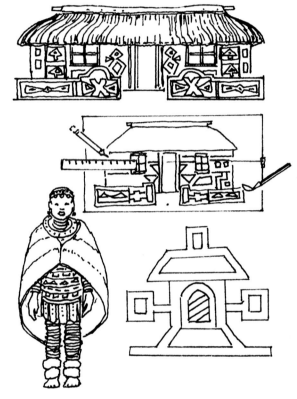

Individual Ndebele housefront

1. This activity lends itself to an individually created housefront as well. After studying the samples of Ndebele houses and walls, the individual will design a house on manila folders or cardboard and display it.
2. The design and production of an Ndebele house is a valid math activity using shapes, color, and symmetry.

In the 16th Century the people known as the Matabele nation lived in this same region. In 1816 they were defeated under the Zulu king Shaka and then by the Boers in 1837. Nyabela, the chief, was imprisoned for life. He encouraged his people to maintain their cultural independence and to continue their ceremonies and traditions though they were "indentured servants" to the surrounding farmers, obliged to serve three months at farm labor each year. When Ndebele girls reach puberty they begin to perfect the arts of beadwork and painting. This is usually taught by mother to daughter. Women have retained their traditional dress with beaded skirts, lavish blanket shawls, and copper leg, arm, and neck rings. Their decorative ingenuity might include mirrors, ostrich feathers, watches, and plastic.

A recommended African book is by Maya Angelou and Margaret Courtney-Clark, *My Painted House, My Friendly Chicken and Me,* Crown Publishing, N.Y., 1994.

KWANZAA DAY CANDELABRA

KWANZAA DAY
CELEBRATION CANDELABRA

Materials: 3 green candles, 3 red candles, 1 black candle, a package of self-hardening clay.

1. Divide the clay into 2 large pieces and set one of them aside. Divide the other into 2 even pieces.

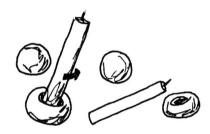

2. From the 2 pieces you just divided, mold 1 of the pieces into seven balls. Turn them into candleholders by inserting the candle in the top of the ball and pressing down. Rotate the candle to make sure the fit is not too tight to remove the candle. Repeat for the other balls of clay.

3. Mold the other piece of clay into a base for the candelabra. Mold the large piece into a foundation for the candle holders.

4. Attach the candleholders and base to the foundation and mold them together. Scratching the surface of the clay (called scoring) helps the pieces stick together. Allow to dry overnight.

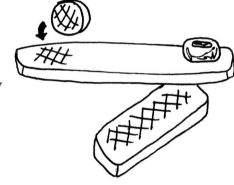

5. Place the colored candles as you see in the photo.

This popular American holiday was first celebrated in 1966 as a celebration of the cultural roots of African Americans. The holiday lasts from December 26 to January 1. "Kwanzaa" means "first fruits" in Swahili and many of the table decorations are foods of the harvest.

The traditional candelabra is called a "kinara". Each candle color is important: black represents the color of the people, red their continuing struggle, and green the color of Mother Africa.

AFRICAN PAPER CHAINS

AFRICAN PAPER CHAINS

Materials: Colored paper, scissors, pencil, water-based paint, markers, glue or tape, patterns on page 76.

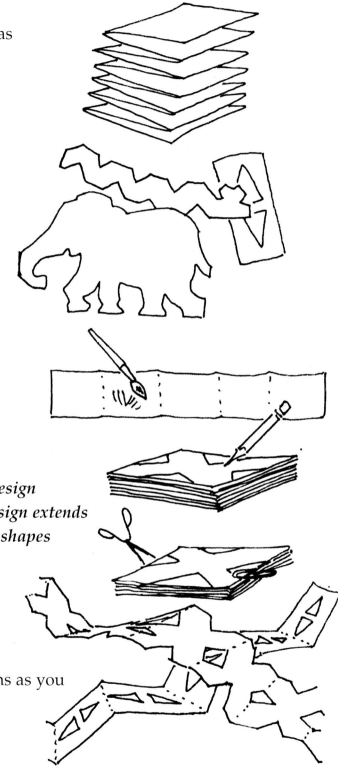

1. Cut the paper into sections 5" to 7" wide and as long as possible.

2. Fold your paper strip accordion-style into 3-4 sections. For a longer paper chain add more paper strips. Cutting this many is about as much as a scissors can cut.

3. Choose a pattern from our pattern page or design your own.

4. If you want to color or paint your paper do so at this time (we sponge painted some of ours to get a texture. They could also be cut out of wrapping paper with an animal pattern or make your own animal pattern). Spread the unfolded paper out and decorate it. Let the painted paper dry before continuing.

5. Refold your decorated paper strip. *Trace the design onto your folded paper strip, making sure the design extends to the folded sides so that when it is cut out the shapes are connected.*

6. Secure your paper for cutting by slipping a paper clip onto a section which will be cut away.

7. Repeat as many of the same or different designs as you wish. Fasten ends of your paper chains together with tape or glue.

Paper chains are used as borders for bulletin boards that present African themes. They have been effectively used as trim on a holiday evergreen that has an African theme. They have also been used as designs for book markers, wrapping paper, cards, invitations, stencils, etc.

AFRICAN ARCHITECTURE

1 NANKANI (GHANA)

2 KANO (NIGERIA)

3 DOGON (MALI)

5 DAHOMEY & BENIN thatch house

4 NIGERIAN MUD HOUSE

10 MASA HOME (CAMEROON)

6 MOSQUE (IVORY COAST)

7 MUD HOUSE (MALI)

8 STORAGE "TANKS" (MALI)

9 MOSQUE (NIGERIA)

MAKING AN AFRICAN HOUSE

Materials: Paper circle about 6", raffia, brown salt dough clay (recipe on page 37) or clay, twigs or craft sticks, scissors and glue.

1. Fold the circle in half and cut halfway into the paper circle. Glue the sides together to make a broad cone.
2. Cut a handful of raffia to 1 1/2". Begin glue-ing a row of raffia at the bottom of the cone. Then glue the middle and top rows, overlapping each row.
3. Form a clay rectangle about 10" long and 2" high. Curve it and leave a door opening.
4. Press sticks into clay for sides to your house and set the thatched roof on top.

WOVEN GRASS BUSHONGO (CONGO) **11**

MASAI (KENYA) **12**

KIKUYU (SUDAN) **13**

MASHONDE (ZIMBABWE) **14**

HIDE HOUSE (SOMALIA) **15**

STONE WALL (GREATER ZIMBABWE) **16**

STONE TOWER (GREATER ZIMBABWE) **16**

NDEBELE (SOUTH AFRICA) **17**

ZULU BEEHIVE (SOUTH AFRICA) **18**

African builders have always been resourceful and creative. Traditional building materials are mud and clay, animal dung, grass or reeds, wood, animal hides, sun-dried brick, and stone.

Many families in Africa live in compounds. These compounds are made up of a central meeting place, separate homes for the householder and each of his wives, cooking and storage areas, and enclosures for animals. A protective fence encircles everything. The Nankani of Ghana create ingenious compounds with structures of mud and dung which the women decorate in dramatic ways with paints from natural dyes. In Benin and Dahomey whole fishing villages of thatch and stick huts perch on stilts high above the water.

Nomadic families in Somalia stretch animal hides over sticks for homes whch can easily be collapsed and loaded onto camels. In the Congo intricately woven mats form beautiful walls for rectangular houses. In South Africa the Zulu cover a framework of tree branches with skillfully plaited grasses to make extraordinary beehive huts, and Ndebele brides cover their homes with bold symmetrical designs. The walls of Greater Zimbabwe are ruins now, but the genius of African architecture survives.

PUPPET, KUBA AND WILD MASK PATTERN

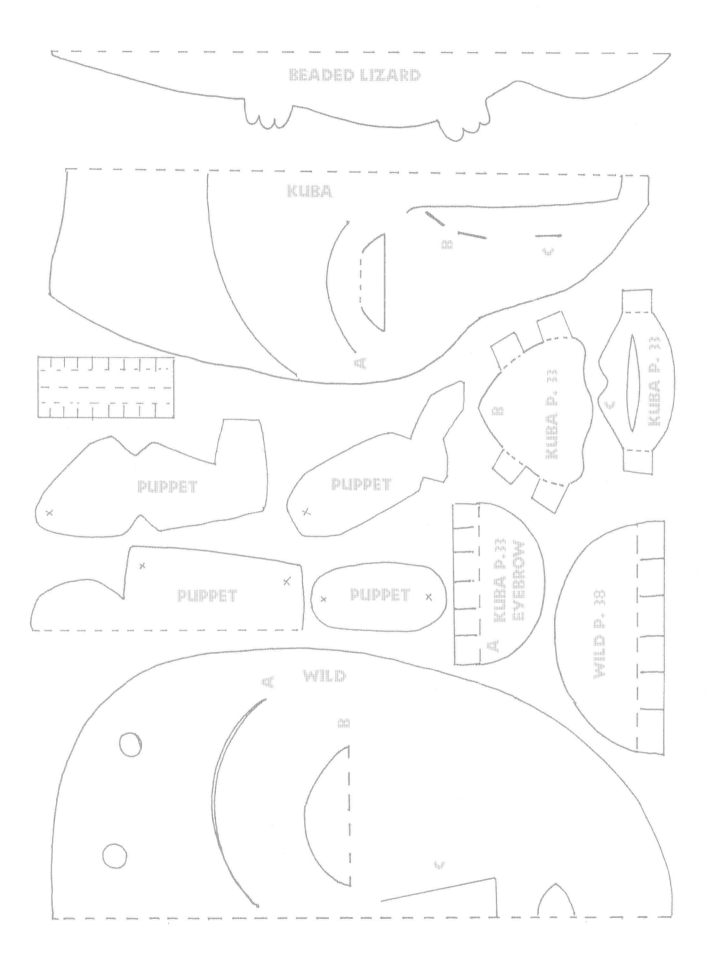

BEADED LIZARD

KUBA

PUPPET

PUPPET

KUBA P. 33

KUBA P. 33

PUPPET

PUPPET

A KUBA P. 33 EYEBROW

WILD P. 38

WILD

SLOTTED ANIMALS

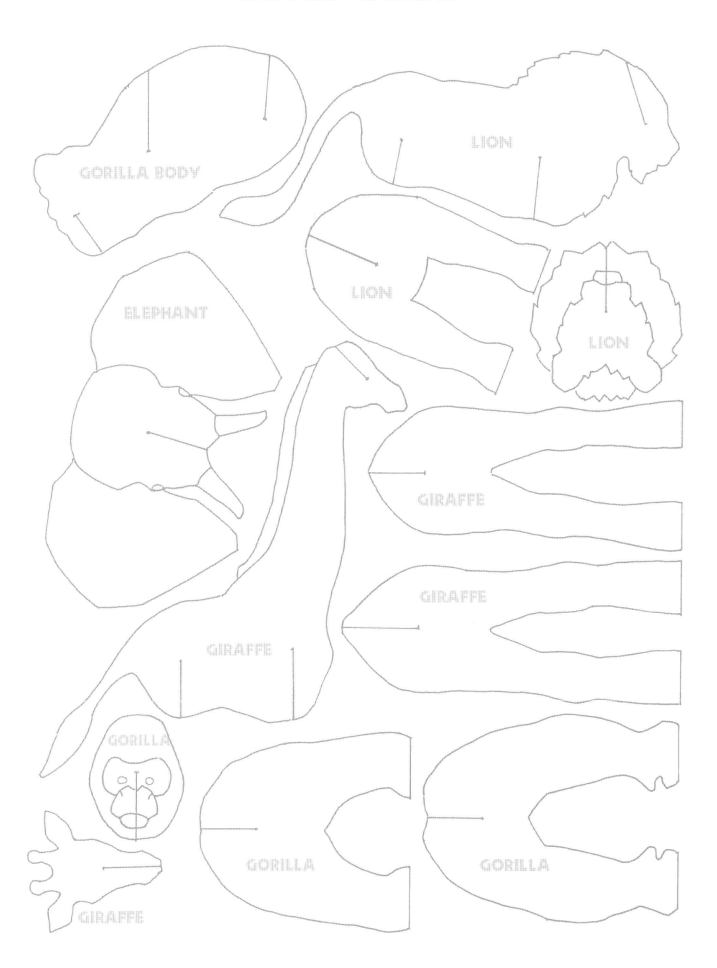

GORILLA BODY

LION

LION

LION

ELEPHANT

GIRAFFE

GIRAFFE

GIRAFFE

GORILLA

GORILLA

GORILLA

GIRAFFE

SLOTTED ANIMALS

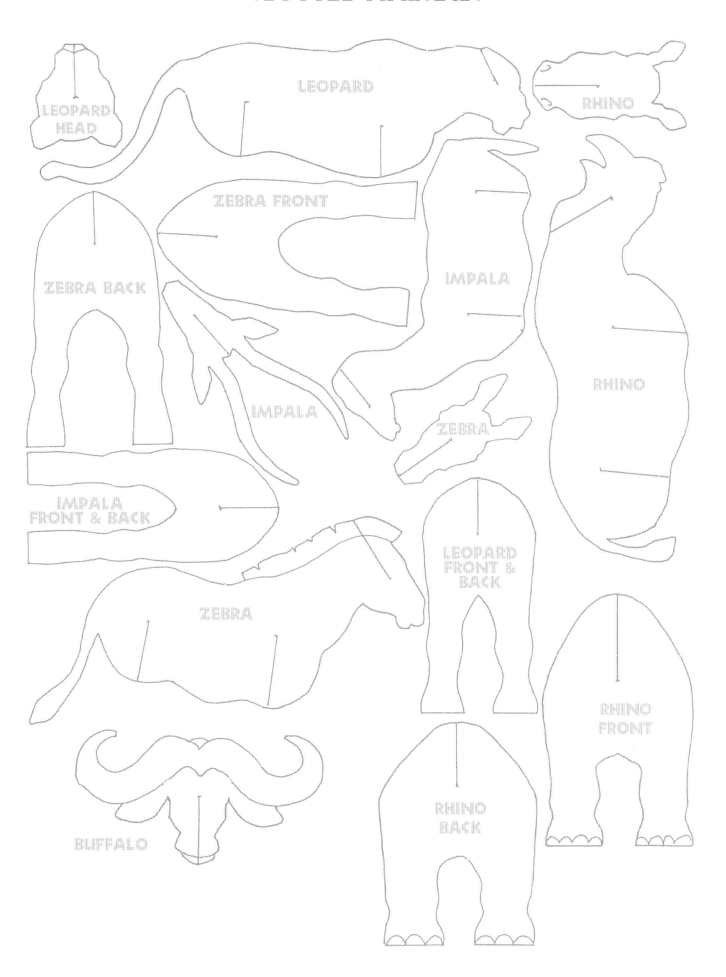

LEOPARD HEAD

LEOPARD

RHINO

ZEBRA FRONT

ZEBRA BACK

IMPALA

RHINO

IMPALA

ZEBRA

IMPALA FRONT & BACK

LEOPARD FRONT & BACK

RHINO FRONT

ZEBRA

BUFFALO

RHINO BACK

SLOTTED ANIMALS

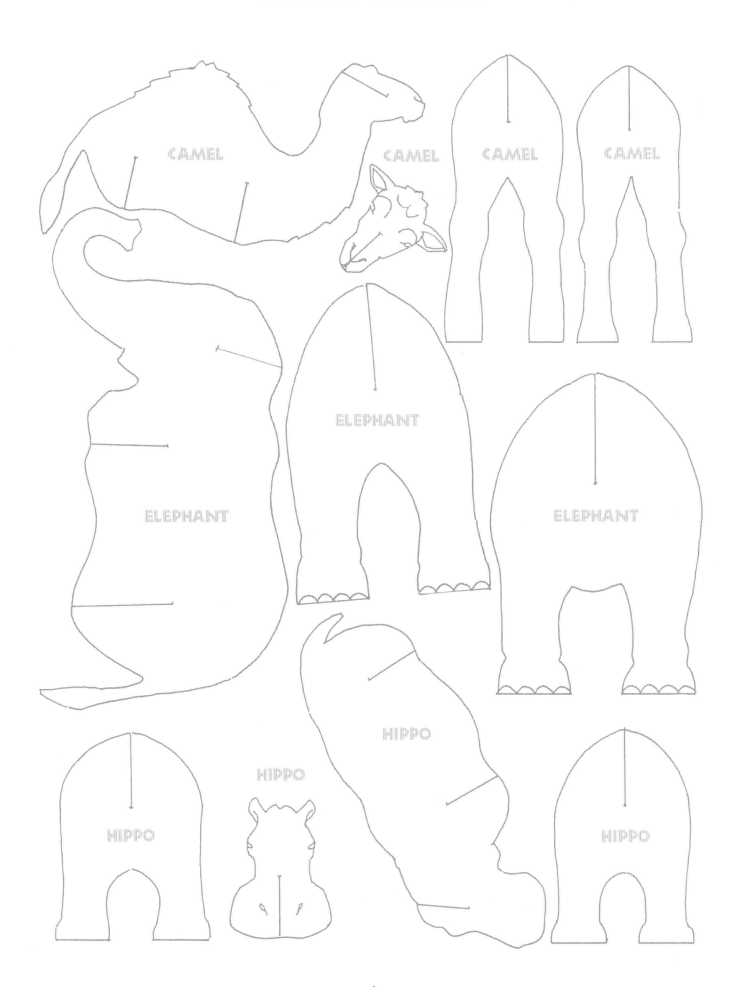

SLOTTED/SCULPTED ANIMALS

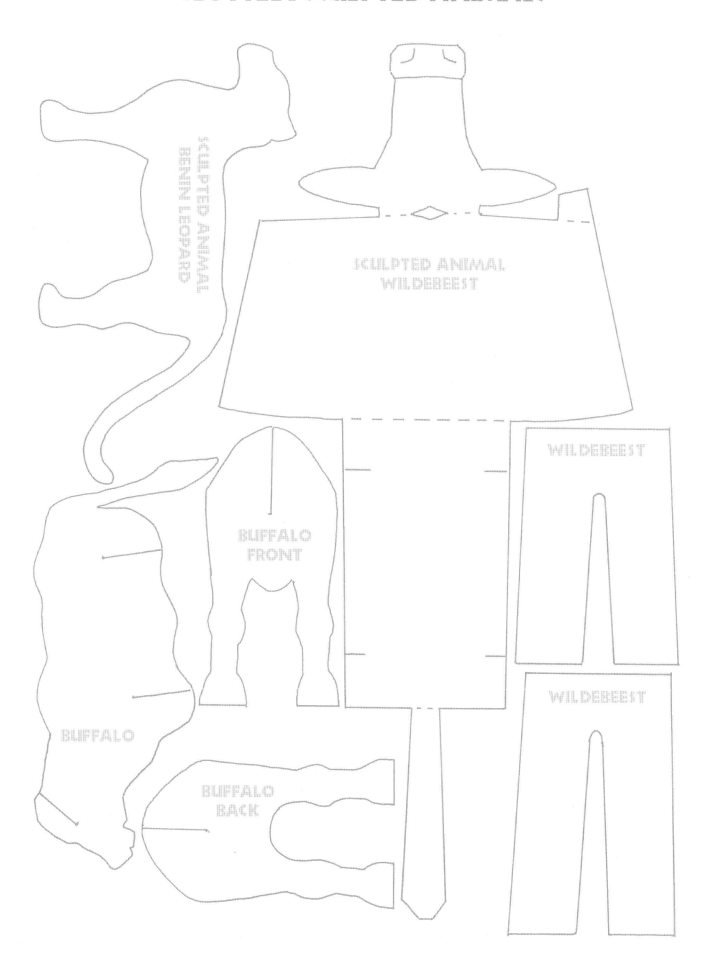

SCULPTED ANIMAL
BENIN LEOPARD

SCULPTED ANIMAL
WILDEBEEST

WILDEBEEST

WILDEBEEST

BUFFALO
FRONT

BUFFALO

BUFFALO
BACK

(Pende Puppet, page 64)

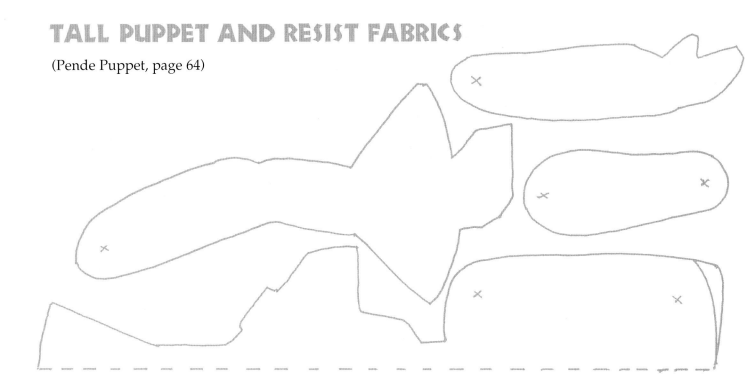

(continued from page 23)

Adire Eleko is designed into sections of your own making and divided by zig zags, dots, wavy lines, etc. After you have "drawn" over your pencil lines with your paste and the paste has dried paint your fabric with a deep blue acrylic paint and proceed as with the mud cloth.

Mud Cloth

1. If you are making mud cloth the designs are bold, geometric, and generally do not represent natural things like birds, fish, etc. See design ideas for mud cloth on page 23.

2. When the paste is thoroughly dry paint your entire fabric with black paint. You can also use ocher (yellowish brown) in places. If you want your cloth to be very, very black paint a second coat

3. After the paint is dry (overnight) wash it off with a hose or in a sink where you can catch the paste mess. Scrape the dried paste off with a spatula or hard-edged tool. How does it look? Let your mud cloth dry.

Adinkra cloth is made by the Ashanti people of Ghana using stamps carved from calabash gourds. The word "Adinkra" means "leaving" and traditionally the cloth was worn only when guests were departing or by people taking part in funerals.

Adire Eleko cloth is made by the Yoruba people in Nigeria who paint over intricate stencils with cassava paste. The dried paste is removed when the cloth is dyed indigo blue. The paste is scrape off and the protected patterns remain white.

Mud cloth is made by the Bambara people of Mali. They dye fabric brown and black and paint lines, circles, zigzags, and oval shapes with a special mud.

CULTURAL PATTERNS

ADINKRA DESIGNS

MOON

ROYALTY

FORGIVENESS

DEFIANCE

THUMB PIANO

CROCODILE

DRUM

BLANKET

SECURITY

FANTÉ FLAG DESIGNS

THUMB PIANO

NDEBELE DESIGNS

THUMB PIANO

83

CULTURAL PATTERNS

WEST AFRICA

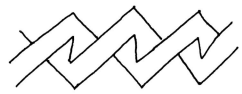

EAST AND CENTRAL AFRICA

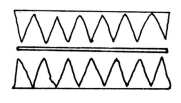

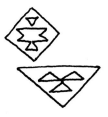

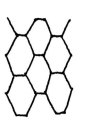

SOUTHERN AFRICA

INDEX

ACKNOWLEDGMENTS

This book has been incubating for five years. My friend **Judith Keller** worked for the Peace Corps in Ghana. When she first saw *Hands-on Alaska* she suggested I consider a similar book on Africa as her special interest was reviving and preserving the folk art in West Africa. My research and musings combined with Judith's knowledge and experience plus her shared collection of artifacts, folk art and textiles finally came together in this publication. Other collectors, educators, and members of the African American community have contributed to the book. **Kay Jones,** the insightful art educator who has contributed to each Hands-on book, shared her African treasures and classroom experiences. **Madlyn Tanner** and **Emily Mortensen** generously edited and proofread the text. **The Bead Connection** is appreciated in the loan of their textiles and objects. **Sister Maryam,** Salt Lake City's favorite African-American storyteller, helped me with information and gathering authentic objects from the African-American community. **Bernadette Brown,** Curator of Education at the Utah Museum of Fine Arts, shared her knowledge and the museum African collection.

BIBLIOGRAPHY

Phillips, Tom, ed. *Africa, The Art of a Continent,* Prestel, N.Y., 1996.
Celebration: A World of Art and Ritual, Renwick Gallery, National Museum of American Art, Smithsonian
    Institution Press, Washington, D.C., 1982.
In Praise of Hands: Contemporary Crafts of the World, World Crafts Council, New York Graphic Society, N.Y., 1974.
Matell, Hazel Mary and Grant Wood, *Exploring Africa,* Peter Bedrick Books, N.Y., 1997.
Schiidkrout, Enid and Keim, *African Reflection,* Univ. of Washington Press, Seattle, 1990.
Miller, Judith Von D., *Art in East Africa,* Africans Publishing Company, N.Y., 1975.
Trowell, Margaret and Hans Neverman, *African and Oceanic Art,* Harry N. Abrams, Inc., N.Y. 1967.
Algotsson, Sharne and Denys Davis, *The Spirit of African Design,* Clarkson Potter Publishers, N.Y., 1996.
Adler, Peter and Nicholas Barnhard, *ASAFO! African Flags of the Fante,* Thames and Hudson, Inc., N.Y., 1992.
Van Offelen, Marion and Carol Beckwith, *Nomads of the Niger,* Harry N. Abrams, N.Y. 1983.
Englebert, Victor, *Wind, Sand and Silence: Travels with Africa's Last Nomads,* Chronicle Books, San Fransisco, 1992.
Fisher, Angela, *Africa Adorned,* Harry N. Abrams, N.Y., 1984.
Nugus-Etienne, Jocelyne, *Crafts and Arts of Living in The Cameroon,* Louisiana State Univ. Press, Baton Rouge, 1982.
Cole, Herbert M., *Ideals and Power in the Art of Africa,* Nat'l. Mus. of African Art, Smithsonian, Washington, D.C., 1989.
Willet, Frank, *African Art,* Thames and Hudson, Inc., N.Y., 1993.
Brill, Marlene, *Libya, Enchantment of the World,* Children's Press, Chicago, 1988.
Fox, Mary Virginia, *Enchantment of West Africa,* Children's Press, Chicago, 1990.
Levy, Patricia, *Nigeria: Cultures of the World,* Marshall Cavendish, N.Y., 1996.
Messner, Julianna, *African Crafts for You to Make,* Simon Schuster, N.Y., 1969.
Corwin, Judith Hoffman, *African Crafts,* Franklin Watts, N.Y., 1998.

RECOMMENDED AFRICAN BOOKS AND STORIES THAT ENHANCE LITERACY

WEST AFRICA
Aardema, Verna and Leo and Diane Dillon, *Why Mosquito Buzzed in People's Ears,* Scholastic Inc., N.Y., 1975.
Aardema, Verna and Joe Cepeda, *Koi and the Kola Nuts,* Atheneum Books, N.Y., 1999.
McDermott, Gerald, *Zomo the Rabbit,* Harcourt, Brace and Jovanovich, San Diego, 1992.
Medearis, Angela Shelf and Terea Shaffer, *The Singing Man,* Holiday House, N.Y., 1994.
Diakite', Baba Wague, *The Hatseller and the Monkeys,* and *The Hunterman and the Crocodile,* Scholastic Press, N.Y., 1999.
Hamilton, Virginia and Barry Moser, *A Ring of Tricksters, African Stories: Cunnie Rabbit etc.,* Scholastic, N.Y., 1997.

CENTRAL AND EAST AFRICA
Aardema, Verna and Beatriz Vidal, *Bringing the Rain to Kapiti Plain,* Dial Books, New York, 1981.

SOUTHERN AFRICA
Steptoe, John, *Mufaro's Beautiful Daughters,* Lothrop, Lee and Shepard Books, N.Y., 1987.
Angelou, Maya and Margaret Courtney-Clark, *My Painted House, My Friendly Chicken and Me,* Crown
    Publishing, N.Y., 1994.
Lester, Julius and David Shannon, *How Many Spots Does A Leopard Have? and other tales,* Scholastic, N.Y., 1989.

Hands-on Alaska
(ISBN 0-9643177-3-7)

Books from
KITS PUBLISHING

Consider these books for:
the library
teaching social studies
art
multicultural programs
ESL programs
museum programs
community youth events
home schooling

Hands-on Rocky Mountains
(ISBN 0-9643177-2-9)

Hands-on Latin America
(ISBN 0-9643177-1-0)

Hands-on Celebrations
(ISBN 0-9643177-4-5)

Hands-on Pioneers
(ISBN 1-57345-085-5)

Hands-on Africa
(ISBN 0-9643177-7-X)

Hands-on Asia
(ISBN 0-9643177-5-3)

ORDER FORM

❒ ____ **Hands-on Africa**

❒ ____ **Hands-on Alaska**

 END TO:_____ PO # _____

❒ ____ **Hands-on Asia**

DDRESS:_____

❒ ____ **Hands-on Celebrations**

❒ ____ **Hands-on Latin America**

TY:_____ STATE:_____ ZIP_____

❒ ____ **Hands-on Pioneers**

ONTACT NAME: _____ PHONE: _____

❒ ____ **Hands-on Rocky Mountains**

_____ Total Quantity Ordered

_____ Shipping and Handling

_____ Total Enclosed/PO

oks are $20⁰⁰ each.

pping and Handling - $3⁰⁰ for the first book
nd $1⁰⁰ for each additional book.
books shipped book rate unless otherwise requested.

Make checks payable to:
KITS PUBLISHING
2359 E. Bryan Avenue • Salt Lake City, Utah 84108
1-801-582-2517 fax: (801) 582-2540
e-mail - info@hands-on.com
Kits Publishing Web site: www.hands-on.com

WORKSHOPS ON AFRICA

Yvonne Merrill is offering **content-strong** workshops for schools, museums, or community programs on the geography, ancient cultures, art, and heritage of Africa.

ALL WORKSHOPS HAVE THESE IMPORTANT ELEMENTS:

*an assessment process
*an interactive and entertaining presentation
*an interdisciplinary emphasis
*a workbook for follow-up activities for instructors
*a menu of offerings organizers can choose according to needs

THE GEOGRAPHY PRESENTATION: Organizers can choose the geography of all of Africa or only West Africa, or East and Central Africa or South Africa. Students explore specific countries, important features and places, ancient history, and modern status.

THE BIOLOGY OF THE REGION: Animals and other natural elements are presented with legend, music, and simple percussion songs.

THE PEOPLE OF THE REGION: Tribes and traditional ceremonies and festivals will be presented. An art project is appropriate here.

Workshops are available January through April starting with the year 2001

1/2 day workshop $250.00   whole-day workshop $500.00

Transportation and lodging are not included • Supplies for art activities are not included
Reservations should be made as early as possible
Maximum number of children in each presentation is 30-40.

THE AFRICAN KIT is also available. It is $500.00 and can be purchased in conjunction with the workshop. A two-hour inservice is an essential part of the kit purchase. The Inservice is $50.00 and is not included in the kit price.

For more information call 801-582-2517, email info@hands-on.com
or check Kits Publishing Web site: www.hands-on.com